The Pontifical Biblical Commission

THE INTERPRETATION
OF THE BIBLE
IN THE CHURCH

*Address of
His Holiness John Paul II and
Document of
The Pontifical Biblical Commission*

BOOKS & MEDIA
BOSTON

ISBN 0-8198-3670-2
(also published by Libreria Editrice Vaticana under
ISBN 88-209-1927-3)

Libreria Editrice Vaticana omnia sibi vindicat iura. Sine eiusdem licentia scripto data nemini liceat hunc. Textum denuo imprimere.

Published in the U.S.A. by Pauline Books & Media, 50 Saint Pauls Avenue, Boston MA 02130-3491. www.pauline.org.

Printed in the U.S.A.

Pauline Books & Media is the publishing house of the Daughters of St. Paul, an international congregation of women religious serving the Church with the communications media.

7 8 9 10 11   10 09 08 07 06

Contents

Address of His Holiness Pope John Paul II

Document of the Pontifical Biblical Commission

His Holiness, Pope John Paul II
Address on the Interpretation
of the Bible in the Church *

This address was given Friday, April 23, 1993, during the course of an audience commemorating the centenary of the encyclical of Leo XIII, "Providentissimus Deus" and the fiftieth anniversary of the encyclical of Pius XII, "Divino Afflante Spiritu," both dedicated to Biblical studies.

The audience was held in the Sala Clementina of the Vatican Palace, in the presence of cardinals, and the Diplomatic Corps accredited to the Holy See, the Pontifical Biblical Commission and professors of the Pontifical Biblical Institute.

During the course of the audience, Cardinal Joseph Ratzinger presented the Pope with the document of the Biblical Commission: The Interpretation of the Bible in the Church.

Your Eminences,
Your Excellencies, the Heads of Diplomatic Missions,
Members of the Pontifical Biblical Commission,
Professors of the Pontifical Biblical Institute,

1. I wholeheartedly thank Cardinal Ratzinger for the sentiments he expressed a few moments ago in presenting the document prepared by the Pontifical Biblical Commission on the Interpretation of the Bible in the Church. I joyfully accept this document, the fruit of a collegial work undertaken on Your

---

* English translation from *L'Osservatore Romano*, weekly edition in English, April 28, 1993, pp. 3, 4, 6. The Holy Father's address was given in French.

document, the fruit of a collegial work undertaken on Your Eminence's initiative, and perseveringly continued over several years. It responds to a heartfelt concern of mine, for the interpretation of Sacred Scripture is of capital importance for the Christian faith and the Church's life. As the Council well reminded us: "In the sacred books the Father who is in heaven comes lovingly to meet his children, and talks with them. And such is the force and power of the word of God that it can serve the Church as her support and vigor, and the children of the Church as strength for their faith, food for the soul, and a pure and lasting source of spiritual life" (*Dei Verbum*, n. 21). For men and women today the manner in which biblical texts are interpreted has immediate consequences for their personal and community relationship with God, and it is also closely connected with the Church's mission. A vital problem is at issue and deserves all your attention.

2. Your work is finishing at a very opportune moment, for it provides me with the opportunity to celebrate with you two richly significant anniversaries: the centenary of the Encyclical *Providentissimus Deus*, and the 50th anniversary of the Encyclical *Divino Afflante Spiritu*, both concerned with biblical questions. On November 18, 1893 Pope Leo XIII, very attentive to intellectual problems, published his encyclical on scriptural studies with the goal, he wrote, "of encouraging and recommending them" as well as "orienting them in a way that better corresponds to the needs of the time" (*Enchiridion Biblicum*, n. 82). Fifty years later, Pope Pius XII gave Catholic exegetes further encouragement and new directives in his encyclical *Divino Afflante Spiritu*. Meanwhile, the papal Magisterium showed its constant concern for scriptural problems through numerous interventions. In 1902 Leo XIII established the Biblical Commission; in 1909 Pius X founded

the Biblical Institute. In 1920 Benedict XV celebrated the 1500th anniversary of St. Jerome's death with an encyclical on the interpretation of the Bible. The strong impetus thus given to biblical studies was fully confirmed at the Second Vatican Council so that the whole Church benefited from it. The Dogmatic Constitution *Dei Verbum* explains the work of Catholic exegetes and invites pastors and the faithful to take greater nourishment from the word of God contained in the Scriptures.

Today I want to highlight some aspects of the teaching of these two encyclicals and the permanent validity of their orientation through changing circumstances, in order to profit more from their contribution.

I. From "Providentissimus Deus" to "Divino Afflante Spiritu"

3. First, one notes an important difference in these two documents, namely, the polemical, or to be more exact, the apologetic part of the two encyclicals. In fact, both appear concerned to answer attacks on the Catholic interpretation of the Bible, but these attacks did not follow the same direction. On the one hand, *Providentissimus Deus* wanted especially to protect Catholic interpretation of the Bible from the attacks of rationalistic science; on the other hand, *Divino Afflante Spiritu* was primarily concerned with defending Catholic interpretation from attacks that opposed the use of science by exegetes and that wanted to impose a non-scientific, so-called "spiritual" interpretation of Sacred Scripture.

This radical change of perspective was obviously due to the circumstances. *Providentissimus Deus* appeared in a period marked by vicious polemics against the Church's faith. Liberal exegesis gave important support to these polemics, for it made use of all the scientific resources, from textual criticism to geology, including philology, literary criticism, history of religions, archaeology and other disciplines besides. On the other hand, *Divino Afflante Spiritu* was published shortly after an entirely different polemic arose, particularly in Italy, against the scientific study of the Bible. An anonymous pamphlet was widely circulated to warn against what it described as "a very serious danger for the Church and souls: the critico-scientific system in the study and interpretation of Sacred Scripture, its disastrous deviations and aberrations."

4. In both cases the reaction of the Magisterium was significant, for instead of giving a purely defensive response, it went to the heart of the problem and thus showed (let us note this at once) the Church's faith in the mystery of the Incarnation.

Against the offensive of liberal exegesis, which presented its allegations as conclusions based on the achievements of science, one could have reacted by anathematizing the use of science in biblical interpretation and ordering Catholic exegetes to hold to a "spiritual" explanation of the texts.

Providentissimus Deus did not take this route. On the contrary, the encyclical earnestly invites Catholic exegetes to acquire genuine scientific expertise so that they may surpass their adversaries in their own field. "The first means of defense," it said, "is found in studying the ancient languages of the East as well as the practice of scientific criticism" (*EB*, n. 118). The Church is not afraid of scientific criticism. She distrusts only preconceived opinions that claim to be based on science, but which in reality surreptitiously cause science to depart from its domain.

Fifty years later in *Divino Afflante Spiritu*, Pope Pius XII could note the fruitfulness of the directives given by

Providentissimus Deus: "Due to a better knowledge of the biblical languages and of everything regarding the East,...a good number of the questions raised at the time of Leo XIII against the authenticity, antiquity, integrity and historical value of the Sacred Books...have now been sorted out and resolved" (*EB*, n. 546). The work of Catholic exegetes "who correctly use the intellectual weapons employed by their adversaries" (n. 562) has borne its fruit. It is for this very reason that *Divino Afflante Spiritu* seems less concerned than *Providentissimus Deus* to fight against the positions of rationalistic exegesis.

5. However, it became necessary to respond to attacks coming from the supporters of a so-called "mystical" exegesis (*EB*, n. 552), who sought to have the Magisterium condemn the efforts of scientific exegesis. How did the encyclical respond? It could have limited itself to stressing the usefulness and even the necessity of these efforts for defending the faith, which would have favored a kind of dichotomy between scientific exegesis, intended for external use, and spiritual interpretation, reserved for internal use. In *Divino Afflante Spiritu*, Pius XII deliberately avoided this approach. On the contrary, he vindicated the close unity of the two approaches, on the one hand emphasizing the "theological" significance of the literal sense, methodically defined (*EB*, n. 551), and on the other, asserting that, to be recognized as the sense of a biblical text, the spiritual sense must offer proof of its authenticity. A merely subjective inspiration is insufficient. One must be able to show that it is a sense "willed by God himself," a spiritual meaning "given by God" to the inspired text (*EB*, nn. 552- 553). Determining the spiritual sense then, belongs itself to the realm of exegetical science.

Thus we note that, despite the great difference in the difficulties they had to face, the two encyclicals are in complete agreement at the deepest level. Both of them reject a split between the human and the divine, between scientific research and respect for the faith, between the literal sense and the spiritual sense. They thus appear to be in perfect harmony with the mystery of the Incarnation.

II. The Harmony between Catholic Exegesis and the Mystery of the Incarnation

6. The strict relationship uniting the inspired biblical texts with the mystery of the incarnation was expressed by the Encyclical *Divino Afflante Spiritu* in the following terms: "Just as the substantial Word of God became like men in every respect except sin, so too the words of God, expressed in human languages, became like human language in every respect except error" (*EB*, n. 559). Repeated almost literally by the conciliar Constitution *Dei Verbum* (n. 13), this statement sheds light on a parallelism rich in meaning.

It is true that putting God's words into writing, through the charism of scriptural inspiration, was the first step toward the incarnation of the Word of God. These written words, in fact, were an abiding means of communication and communion between the chosen people and their one Lord. On the other hand, it is because of the prophetic aspect of these words that it was possible to recognize the fulfillment of God's plan when "the Word became flesh and made his dwelling among us" (*Jn* 1:14). After the heavenly glorification of the humanity of the Word made flesh, it is again due to written words that his stay among us is attested to in an abiding way. Joined to the inspired writings of the first covenant, the inspired writings of the new covenant are a verifiable means of communication and communion between the believing people and God, the Father, Son and Holy Spirit. This means certainly can never be separated from the stream of spiritual life that flows from the Heart of Jesus crucified and which spreads through the Church's sacraments. It has nevertheless its own consistency precisely as a written text which verifies it.

7. Consequently, the two encyclicals require that Catholic exegetes remain in full harmony with the mystery of the Incarnation, a mystery of the union of the divine and the human in a determinate historical life. The earthly life of Jesus is not defined only by the places and dates at the beginning of the 1st century in Judea and Galilee, but also by his deep roots in the long history of a small nation of the ancient Near East, with its weaknesses and its greatness, with its men of God and its sinners, with its slow cultural evolution and its political misadventures, with its defeats and its victories, with its longing for peace and the kingdom of God. The Church of Christ takes the realism of the incarnation seriously, and this is why she attaches great importance to the "historico-critical" study of the Bible. Far from condemning it, as those who support "mystical" exegesis would want, my predecessors vigorously approved. "Artis criticae disciplinam," Leo XIII wrote, "quippe percipiendae penitus hagiographorum sententiae perutilem, *Nobis vehementer probantibus*, nostri (exegetae, scilicet, catholici) excolant" (Apostolic Letter *Vigilantiae*, establishing the Biblical Commission, October 30, 1902: *EB*, n. 142). The same "vehemence" in the approval and the same adverb ("vehementer") are found in *Divino Afflante Spiritu* regarding research in textual criticism (cf *EB*, n. 548).

8. *Divino Afflante Spiritu*, we know, particularly recommended that exegetes study the *literary genres* used in the Sacred Books, going so far as to say that Catholic exegesis must "be convinced that this part of its task cannot be neglected without serious harm to Catholic exegesis" (*EB*, n. 560). This recommendation starts from the concern to understand the

meaning of the texts with all the accuracy and precision possible and, thus, in their historical, cultural context. A false idea of God and the incarnation presses a certain number of Christians to take the opposite approach. They tend to believe that, since God is the absolute Being, each of his words has an absolute value, independent of all the conditions of human language. Thus, according to them, there is no room for studying these conditions in order to make distinctions that would relativize the significance of the words. However, that is where the illusion occurs and the mysteries of scriptural inspiration and the incarnation are really rejected, by clinging to a false notion of the Absolute. The God of the Bible is not an absolute Being who, crushing everything he touches, would suppress all differences and all nuances. On the contrary, he is God the Creator, who created the astonishing variety of beings "each according to its kind," as the *Genesis* account says repeatedly (*Gn* 1). Far from destroying differences, God respects them and makes use of them (cf *1 Cor* 12:18, 24, 28). Although he expresses himself in human language, he does not give each expression a uniform value, but uses its possible nuances with extreme flexibility and likewise accepts its limitations. That is what makes the task of exegetes so complex, so necessary and so fascinating! None of the human aspects of language can be neglected. The recent progress in linguistic, literary and hermeneutical research have led biblical exegesis to add many other points of view (rhetorical, narrative, structuralist) to the study of literary genres; other human sciences, such as psychology and sociology, have likewise been employed. To all this one can apply the charge which Leo XIII gave the members of the Biblical Commission: "Let them consider nothing that the diligent research of modern scholars will have newly found as foreign to their realm; quite the contrary, let them be alert to adopt without delay anything useful that each period brings to biblical exegesis" (*Vigilantiae*: *EB* n. 140). Studying the human circumstances of the word of God should be pursued with ever renewed interest.

9. Nevertheless, this study is not enough. In order to respect the coherence of the Church's faith and of scriptural inspiration, Catholic exegesis must be careful not to limit itself to the human aspects of the biblical texts. First and foremost, it must help the Christian people more dearly perceive the word of God in these texts so that they can better accept them in order to live in full communion with God. To this end it is obviously necessary that the exegete himself perceive the divine word in the texts. He can do this only if his intellectual work is sustained by a vigorous spiritual life.

Without this support, exegetical research remains incomplete; it loses sight of its main purpose and is confined to secondary tasks. It can even become a sort of escape. Scientific study of the merely human aspects of the texts can make the exegete forget that the word of God invites each person to come out of himself to live in faith and love.

On this point the Encyclical *Providentissimus Deus* recalls the special nature of the Sacred Books and their consequent need for interpretation: "The Sacred Books," he said, "cannot be likened to ordinary writings, but, since they have been dictated by the Holy Spirit himself and have extremely serious contents, mysterious and difficult in many respects, we always need, in order to understand and explain them, the coming of the same Holy Spirit, that is, his light and grace, which must certainly be sought in humble prayer and preserved by a life of holiness" (*EB*, n. 89). In a shorter formula, borrowed from St. Augustine, *Divino Afflante Spiritu* expressed the same requirement: "Orent ut intelligant!" (*EB*, n. 569).

Indeed, to arrive at a completely valid interpretation of

words inspired by the Holy Spirit, one must first be guided by the Holy Spirit and it is necessary to pray for that, to pray much, to ask in prayer for the interior light of the Spirit and docilely accept that light, to ask for the love that alone enables one to understand the language of God, who "is love" (*1 Jn* 4:8, 16). While engaged in the very work of interpretation, one must remain in the presence of God as much as possible.

10. Docility to the Holy Spirit produces and reinforces another attitude needed for the correct orientation of exegesis: fidelity to the Church. The Catholic exegete does not entertain the individualist illusion leading to the belief that one can better understand the biblical texts outside the community of believers. The contrary is true, for these texts have not been given to individual researchers "to satisfy their curiosity or provide them with subjects for study and research" (*Divino Afflante Spiritu*: *EB*, n. 566); they have been entrusted to the community of believers, to the Church of Christ, in order to nourish faith and guide the life of charity. Respect for this purpose conditions the validity of the interpretation. *Providentissimus Deus* recalled this basic truth and observed that, far from hampering biblical research, respect for this fact fosters its authentic progress (cf *EB*, nn. 108-109). It is comforting to note that recent studies in hermeneutical philosophy have confirmed this point of view and that exegetes of various confessions have worked from similar perspectives by stressing, for example, the need to interpret each biblical text as part of the scriptural canon recognized by the Church, or by being more attentive to the contributions of patristic exegesis.

Being faithful to the Church, in fact, means resolutely finding one's place in the mainstream of the great Tradition that, under the guidance of the Magisterium, assured of the Holy Spirit's special assistance, has recognized the canonical writings as the word addressed by God to his people and has never ceased meditating on them and discovering their inexhaustible riches. The Second Vatican Council asserted this again: "All that has been said about the manner of interpreting Scripture is ultimately subject to the judgment of the Church, which exercises the divinely conferred commission and ministry of watching over and interpreting the word of God" (*Dei Verbum*, n. 12).

It is nevertheless true — the Council also states this, repeating an assertion of *Providentissimus Deus* — that it "is the task of exegetes to work, according to these rules, toward a better understanding and explanation of the meaning of Sacred Scripture in order that their research may help the Church to form a firmer judgment" (*Dei Verbum*, n. 12; cf *Providentissimus Deus: EB*, n. 109: "ut, quasi praeparato studio, iudicium Ecclesiae maturetur").

11. In order to carry out this very important ecclesial task better, exegetes will be keen to remain close to the preaching of God's word, both by devoting part of their time to this ministry and by maintaining relations with those who exercise it and helping them with publications of pastoral exegesis (cf *Divino Afflante Spiritu: EB*, n. 551). Thus they will avoid becoming lost in the complexities of abstract scientific research which distances them from the true meaning of the Scriptures. Indeed, this meaning is inseparable from their goal, which is to put believers into a personal relationship with God.

III. The New Document of the Biblical Commission

12. In these perspectives, *Providentissimus Deus* stated, "a vast field of research is open to the personal work of each exegete" (*EB*, n. 109). Fifty years later, *Divino Afflante Spiritu* again made the same encouraging observation: "There are still many points, some very important, in the discussion

and explanation of which the intellectual penetration and talent of Catholic exegetes can and should be freely exercised" (*EB*, n. 565).

What was true in 1943 remains so even in our day, for advances in research have produced solutions to certain problems and, at the same time, new questions to be studied. In exegesis, as in other sciences, the more one pushes back the limits of the unknown, the more one enlarges the area to be explored. Less than five years after the publication of *Divino Afflante Spiritu*, the discovery of the Qumran scrolls shed the light of a new day on a great number of biblical problems and opened up other fields of research. Since then, many discoveries have been made and new methods of investigation and analysis have been perfected.

13. It is this changed situation that has made a new examination of the problems necessary. The Pontifical Biblical Commission has worked on this task and today presents the fruit of its work, entitled *L'interprétation de la Bible dans l'Église*.

What is striking on first reading this document is the *spirit of openness* in which it was conceived. The methods, approaches and interpretations practiced today in exegesis have been examined and, despite occasionally serious reservations which must be stated, one acknowledges in almost every case, the presence of valid elements for an integral interpretation of the biblical text.

For Catholic exegesis does not have its own exclusive method of interpretation, but starting with the historico-critical basis freed from its philosophical presuppositions or those contrary to the truth of our faith, it makes the most of all the current methods by seeking in each of them the "seeds of the Word."

14. Another characteristic feature of this synthesis is its

balance and moderation. In its interpretation of the Bible, it knows how to harmonize the diachronic and the synchronic by recognizing that the two are mutually complementary and indispensable for bringing out all the truth of the text and for satisfying the legitimate demands of the modern reader.

Even more importantly, Catholic exegesis does not focus its attention on only the human aspects of biblical Revelation, which is sometimes the mistake of the historico-critical method, or on only the divine aspects, as fundamentalism would have it; it strives to highlight both of them as they are united in the divine "condescension" (*Dei Verbum*, n. 13), which is the basis of all Scripture.

15. Lastly, one will perceive the document's stress on the fact that *the biblical Word is at work speaking universally, in time and space*, to all humanity. If "the words of God...are like human language" (*Dei Verbum*, n. 13), it is so that they may be understood by all. They must not remain distant, "too mysterious and remote for you.... For the word is very near to you, already in your mouths and in your hearts; you have only to carry it out" (*Dt* 30:11, 14).

This is the aim of biblical interpretation. If the first task of exegesis is to arrive at the authentic sense of the sacred text or even at its different senses, it must then communicate this meaning to the recipient of Sacred Scripture, who is every human person, if possible.

The Bible exercises its influence down the centuries. A constant process of actualization adapts the interpretation to the contemporary mentality and language. The concrete, immediate nature of biblical language greatly facilitates this adaptation, but its origin in an ancient culture causes not a few difficulties. Therefore, biblical thought must always be translated anew into contemporary language so that it may be expressed in ways suited to its listeners. This translation, however, should be faithful to the original and cannot force the texts in order to accommodate an interpretation or an approach fashionable at a given time. The word of God must appear in all its splendor, even if it is "expressed in human words" (*Dei Verbum*, n. 13).

Today the Bible has spread to every continent and every nation. However, in order for it to have a profound effect, there must be *inculturation* according to the genius proper to each people. Perhaps nations less marked by the deviances of modern Western civilization will understand the biblical message more easily than those who are already insensitive as it were to the action of God's word because of secularization and the excesses of de-mythologization.

In our day, a great effort is necessary, not only on the part of scholars and preachers, but also those who popularize biblical thought: they should use every means possible — and there are many today — so that the universal significance of the biblical message may be widely acknowledged and its saving efficacy may be seen everywhere.

Thanks to this document, the interpretation of the Bible in the Church will be able to obtain new vigor for the good of the whole world, so that the truth may shine forth and stir up charity on the threshold of the third millennium.

Conclusion

16. Finally, I have the joy as my predecessors, Leo XIII and Pius XII had, of being able to offer to Catholic exegetes, and in particular, to you, the members of the Pontifical Biblical Commission, both my thanks and encouragement.

I cordially thank you for the excellent work you have accomplished in service to the word of God and the People of

God: a work of research, teaching and publication; an aid to theology, to the liturgy of the word and to the ministry of preaching; initiatives fostering ecumenism and good relations between Christians and Jews; involvement in the Church's efforts to respond to the aspirations and difficulties of the modern world.

To this I add my warm encouragement for the next step to be taken. The increasing complexity of the task requires everyone's effort and a broad interdisciplinary cooperation. In a world where scientific research is taking on greater importance in many domains, it is indispensable for exegetical science to find its place at a comparable level. It is one of the aspects of inculturating the faith which is part of the Church's mission in connection with accepting the mystery of the Incarnation.

May you be guided in your research by Jesus Christ, the incarnate Word of God, who opened the minds of his disciples to the understanding of the Scriptures (*Lk* 24:45). May the Virgin Mary serve as a model for you not only by her generous docility to the word of God, but also and especially by her way of accepting what was said to her! St. Luke tells us that Mary reflected in her heart on the divine words and the events that took place, "symbállousa en tê kardía autês" (*Lk* 2:19). By welcoming the Word she is the model and mother of disciples (cf *Jn* 19:27). Therefore, may she teach you fully to accept the word of God, not only in intellectual research but also with your whole life!

In order that your work and your activity may make the light of the Scriptures shine ever more brightly, I wholeheartedly give you my Apostolic Blessing.

Pontifical Bibilical Commission

The Interpretation of the Bible in the Church

Translated from the French by
John Kilgallen and Brendan Byrne

Preface by Cardinal Joseph Ratzinger

The study of the Bible is, as it were, the soul of theology, as the Second Vatican Council says, borrowing a phrase from Pope Leo XIII (*DV* 24). This study is never finished; each age must in its own way newly seek to understand the sacred books. In the history of interpretation the rise of the historical-critical method opened a new era. With it, new possibilities for understanding the biblical word in its originality opened up. Just as with all human endeavor, though, so also this method contained hidden dangers along with its positive possibilities: the search for the original can lead to putting the word back into the past completely so that it is no longer taken in its actuality. It can result that only the human dimension of the word appears as real, while the genuine author, God, is removed from the reach of a method which was established for understanding human reality. The application of a "profane" method to the Bible necessarily led to discussion. Everything that helps us better to understand the truth and to appropriate its representations is helpful and worthwhile for theology. It is in this sense that we must seek how to use this method in theological research. Everything that shrinks our horizon and hinders us from seeing and hearing beyond that which is merely human must be opened up. Thus the emergence of the historical-critical method set in motion at the same time a struggle over its scope and over its proper configuration which is by no means finished as yet.

In this struggle the teaching office of the Catholic Church has taken up positions several times. First, Pope Leo XIII, in his encyclical *Providentissimus Deus* of November 18, 1893, plotted out some markers on the exegetical map. At a time when liberalism was extremely sure of itself and much too intrusively dogmatic, Leo XIII was forced to express himself in a rather critical way, even though he did not exclude that which was positive from the new possibilities. Fifty years later, however, because of the fertile work of great Catholic exegetes, Pope Pius XII, in his encyclical *Divino Afflante Spiritu* of September 30, 1943, was able to provide largely positive encouragement toward making the modern methods of understanding the Bible fruitful. The Constitution on Divine Revelation of the Second Vatican Council, *Dei Verbum*, of November 18, 1965, adopted all of this. It provided us with a synthesis, which substantially remains, between the lasting insights of patristic theology and the new methodological understanding of the moderns.

In the meantime, this methodological spectrum of exegetical work has broadened in a way which could not have been envisioned thirty years ago. New methods and new approaches have appeared, from structuralism to materialistic, psychoanalytic and liberation exegesis. On the other hand, there are also new attempts to recover patristic exegesis and to include renewed forms of a spiritual interpretation of scripture. Thus the Pontifical Biblical Commission took as its task an attempt to take the bearings of Catholic exegesis in the present situation one hundred years after *Providentissimus Deus* and fifty years after *Divino Afflante Spiritu*. The Pontifical Biblical Commission, in its new form after the Second Vatican Council, is not an organ of the teaching office, but rather a commission of scholars who, in their scientific and ecclesial responsibility as believing exegetes, take positions on important problems of Scriptural interpretation and know that for this task they enjoy the confidence of the teaching office. Thus the present document was established. It contains a well-grounded overview of the panorama of present-day methods and in this way offers to the inquirer an orientation to the possibilities and limits of these approaches. Accordingly, the text of the document inquires into how the meaning of Scripture might become known — this meaning in which the human word and God's word work together in the singularity of historical events and the eternity of the everlasting Word which is contemporary in every age. The biblical word comes from a real past. It comes not only from the past, however, but at the same time from the eternity of God and it leads us into God's eternity, but again along the way through time, to which the past, the present and the future belong. I believe that this document is very helpful for the important questions about the right way of understanding Holy Scripture, and that it also helps us to go further. It takes up the paths of the encyclicals of 1893 and 1943 and advances them in a fruitful way. I would like to thank the members of the Biblical Commission for the patient and frequently laborious struggle in which this text grew little by little. I hope that the document will have a wide circulation so that it becomes a genuine contribution to the search for a deeper assimilation of the word of God in Holy Scripture.

Rome, on the feast of St. Matthew the Evangelist 1993.
JOSEPH Cardinal RATZINGER

Introduction

The interpretation of biblical texts continues in our own day to be a matter of lively interest and significant debate. In recent years the discussions involved have taken on some new dimensions. Granted the fundamental importance of the Bible for Christian faith, for the life of the Church and for relations between Christians and the faithful of other religions, the Pontifical Biblical Commission has been asked to make a statement on this subject.

A. The State of the Question Today

The problem of the interpretation of the Bible is hardly a modern phenomenon, even if at times that is what some would have us believe. The Bible itself bears witness that its interpretation can be a difficult matter. Alongside texts that are perfectly clear, it contains passages of some obscurity. When reading certain prophecies of Jeremiah, Daniel pondered at length over their meaning (*Dn* 9:2). According to the *Acts of the Apostles*, an Ethiopian of the 1st century found himself in the same situation with respect to a passage from the book of *Isaiah* (*Isa* 53:7-8) and recognized that he had need of an interpreter (*Acts* 8:30-35). The *Second Letter of Peter* insists that "no prophecy of Scripture is a matter of private interpretation" (*2 Pet* 1:20) and it also observes that the letters of the Apostle Paul contain "some difficult passages, the meaning of which the ignorant and untrained distort, as they do also in the case of the other Scriptures, to their own ruin" (*2 Pet* 3:16).

The problem is, therefore, quite old. But it has been accentuated with the passage of time. Readers today, in order to appropriate the words and deeds of which the Bible speaks, have to project themselves back almost twenty or thirty centuries — a process which always creates difficulty. Furthermore, because of the progress made in the human sciences, questions of interpretation have become more complex in modern times. Scientific methods have been adopted for the study of the texts of the ancient world. To what extent can these methods be considered appropriate for the interpretation of Holy Scripture? For a long period the Church in her pastoral prudence showed herself very reticent in responding to this question, for often the methods, despite their positive elements, have shown themselves to be wedded to positions hostile to the Christian faith. But a more positive attitude has also evolved, signaled by a whole series of pontifical documents, ranging from the encyclical *Providentissimus Deus* of Leo XIII (Nov. 18, 1893) to the encyclical *Divino Afflante Spiritu* of Pius XII (Sept. 30, 1943) and this has been confirmed by the Declaration *Sancta Mater Ecclesia* of the Pontifical Biblical Commission (April 21, 1964) and above all by the Dogmatic Constitution *Dei Verbum* of the Second Vatican Council (Nov. 18, 1965).

That this more constructive attitude has borne fruit cannot be denied. Biblical studies have made great progress in the Catholic Church and the academic value of these studies has been acknowledged more and more in the scholarly world and among the faithful. This has greatly smoothed the path of ecumenical dialogue. The deepening of the Bible's influence upon theology has contributed to theological renewal. Interest in the Bible has grown among Catholics, with resultant progress in the Christian life. All those who have acquired a solid formation in this area consider it quite impossible to return to a precritical level of interpretation, a level which they now rightly judge to be quite inadequate.

But the fact is that at the very time when the most prevalent scientific method — the "historical-critical method" — is freely practiced in exegesis, including Catholic exegesis, it is itself *brought into question*. To some extent, this has come about in the scholarly world itself, through the rise of alternative methods and approaches. But it has also arisen through the criticisms of many members of the faithful, who judge the method deficient from the point of view of faith. The historical-critical method, as its name suggests, is particularly attentive to the historical development of texts or traditions across the passage of time — that is, to all that is summed up by the term *"diachronic."* But at the present time in certain quarters it finds itself in competition with methods which insist upon a *synchronic* understanding of texts — that is, one which has to do with their language, composition, narrative structure and capacity for persuasion. Moreover, for many interpreters the diachronic concern to reconstruct the past has given way to a tendency to ask questions of texts by viewing them within a number of contemporary perspectives — philosophical, psychoanalytic, sociological, political, etc. Some value this plurality of methods and approaches as an indication of richness, but to others it gives the impression of much confusion.

Whether real or apparent, this confusion has brought fresh fuel to the arguments of those opposed to scientific exegesis. The diversity of interpretations only serves to show, they say, that nothing is gained by submitting biblical texts to the demands of scientific method; on the contrary, they allege, much is lost thereby. They insist that the result of scientific exegesis is only to provoke perplexity and doubt upon numerous points which hitherto had been accepted without difficulty. They add that it impels some exegetes to adopt positions contrary to the faith of the Church on matters of great importance, such as the virginal conception of Jesus and his miracles, and even his resurrection and divinity.

Even when it does not end up in such negative positions,

scientific exegesis, they claim, is notable for its sterility in what concerns progress in the Christian life. Instead of making for easier and more secure access to the living sources of God's Word, it makes of the Bible a closed book. Interpretation may always have been something of a problem, but now it requires such technical refinements as to render it a domain reserved for a few specialists alone. To the latter some apply the phrase of the gospel: "You have taken away the key of knowledge; you have not entered in yourselves, and you have hindered those who sought to enter" (*Luke* 11:52; cf *Matt* 23:13).

As a result, in place of the patient toil of scientific exegesis, they think it necessary to substitute simpler approaches, such as one or other of the various forms of synchronic reading which may be considered appropriate. Some even, turning their backs upon all study, advocate a so-called "spiritual" reading of the Bible, by which they understand a reading guided solely by personal inspiration — one that is subjective — and intended only to nourish such inspiration. Some seek above all to find in the Bible the Christ of their own personal vision and, along with it, the satisfaction of their own spontaneous religious feelings. Others claim to find there immediate answers to all kinds of questions, touching both their own lives and that of the community. There are, moreover, numerous sects which propose as the only way of interpretation one that has been revealed to them alone.

B. The Purpose of this Document

It is, then, appropriate to give serious consideration to the various aspects of the present situation as regards the interpretation of the Bible — to attend to the criticisms and the complaints, as also to the hopes and aspirations which are being expressed in this matter, to assess the possibilities opened up by the new methods and approaches and, finally, to try to determine more precisely the direction which best corresponds to the mission of exegesis in the Catholic Church.

Such is the purpose of this document. The Pontifical Biblical Commission desires to indicate the paths most appropriate for arriving at an interpretation of the Bible as faithful as possible to its character both human and divine. The Commission does not aim to adopt a position on all the questions which arise with respect to the Bible — such as, for example, the theology of inspiration. What it has in mind is to examine all the methods likely to contribute effectively to the task of making more available the riches contained in the biblical texts. The aim is that the Word of God may become more and more the spiritual nourishment of the members of the People of God, the source for them of a life of faith, of hope and of love — and indeed a light for all humanity (cf *Dei Verbum*, 21).

To accomplish this goal, the present document:

1. will give a brief description of the various methods and approaches,[1] indicating the possibilities they offer and their limitations;

2. will examine certain questions of a hermeneutical nature;

3. will reflect upon the aspects which may be considered characteristic of a Catholic interpretation of the Bible and upon its relationship with other theological disciplines;

4. will consider, finally, the place interpretation of the Bible has in the life of the Church.

---

1. By an exegetical "method" we understand a group of scientific procedures employed in order to explain texts. We speak of an "approach" when it is a question of an enquiry proceeding from a particular point of view.

I. Methods and Approaches for Interpretation

A. The Historical-Critical Method

The historical-critical method is the indispensable method for the scientific study of the meaning of ancient texts. Holy Scripture, inasmuch as it is the "Word of God in human language," has been composed by human authors in all its various parts and in all the sources that lie behind them. Because of this, its proper understanding not only admits the use of this method but actually requires it.

1. History of the Method

For a correct understanding of this method as currently employed, a glance over its history will be of assistance. Certain elements of this method of interpretation are very ancient. They were used in antiquity by Greek commentators of classical literature and, much later, in the course of the Patristic period, by authors such as Origen, Jerome and Augustine. The method at that time was much less developed. Its modern forms are the result of refinements brought about especially since the time of the Renaissance humanists and their *recursus ad fontes* (return to the sources). The *textual criticism* of the New Testament was able to be developed as a scientific discipline only from about 1800 onwards, after its link with the *Textus receptus* was severed. But the beginnings of *literary criticism* go back to the 17th century, to the work of Richard Simon, who drew attention to the doublets, discrepancies in content and differences of style observable in the Pentateuch — discoveries not easily to reconcile with the attribution of the entire text to Moses as single author. In the 18th century, Jean Astruc was still satisfied that the matter could be explained on the basis that Moses had made use of various sources (especially two principal ones) to compose the Book of *Genesis*. But as time passed biblical critics contested the Mosaic authorship of the Pentateuch with ever growing confidence. Literary criticism for a long time came to be identified with the attempt to distinguish in texts different sources. Thus it was that there developed in the 19th century the "Documentary Hypothesis," which sought to give an explanation of the editing of the Pentateuch. According to this hypothesis, four documents, to some extent parallel with each other, had been woven together: that of the Yahwist (J), that of the Elohist (E), the Deuteronomy (D) and that of the Priestly Author (P); the final editor made use of this latter (Priestly) document to provide a structure for the whole. In similar fashion, to explain both the agreements and disagreements between the three Synoptic Gospels, scholars had recourse to the "Two Source" Hypothesis. According to this, the Gospels of *Matthew* and *Luke* were composed out of two principal sources: on the one hand, the Gospel of *Mark* and, on the other, a collection of the sayings of Jesus (called "Q," from the German word *"Quelle,"* meaning "source"). In their essential features, these two hypotheses retain their prominence in scientific exegesis today — though they are also under challenge.

In the desire to establish the chronology of the biblical texts, this kind of literary criticism restricted itself to the task of dissecting and dismantling the text in order to identify the various sources. It did not pay sufficient attention to the final form of the biblical text and to the message which it conveyed in the state in which it actually exists (the contribution of editors was not held in high regard). This meant that historical-critical exegesis could often seem to be something which simply dissolved and destroyed the text. This was all the more the case when, under the influence of the comparative history of religions, such as it then was, or on the basis of certain philosophical ideas, some exegetes expressed highly negative judgments against the Bible.

It was Hermann Gunkel who brought the method out of the ghetto of literary criticism understood in this way. Although he continued to regard the books of the Pentateuch as compilations, he attended to the particular texture of the different elements of the text. He sought to define the genre of each piece (e.g., whether "legend" or "hymn") and its original setting in the life of the community or *"Sitz im Leben"* (e.g., a legal setting, or a liturgical one, etc.). To this kind of research into literary genres was joined the "critical study of forms" *("Formgeschichte"),* which Martin Dibelius and Rudolf Bultmann introduced into the exegesis of the Synoptic Gospels. Bultmann combined form-critical studies with a biblical hermeneutic inspired by the existentialist philosophy of Martin Heidegger. As a result, *Formgeschichte* often stirred up serious reservations. But one of the results of this method has been to demonstrate more clearly that the tradition recorded in the New Testament had its origin and found its basic shape within Christian community, or early Church, passing from the preaching of Jesus himself to that which proclaimed that Jesus is the Christ. Eventually, form-criticism was supplemented by *"Redaktionsgeschichte"* ("redaction-criticism"), the "critical study of the process of editing." This sought to shed light upon the personal contribution of each evangelist and to uncover the theological tendencies which shaped his editorial work. When this last method was brought into play, the whole series of different stages characteristic of the historical-critical method became complete: from textual criticism one progresses to literary criticism, with its work of dissection in the quest for sources; then one moves to a critical study of forms and, finally, to an analysis of the editorial process, which aims to be particularly attentive to the text as it has been put together. All this has made it possible to understand far more accurately the intention of the authors and editors of the Bible, as well as the message which they addressed to their first readers. The achievement of these results has lent the historical-critical method an importance of the highest order.

2. *Principles*

The fundamental principles of the historical-critical method in its classic form are the following:

It is a *historical* method, not only because it is applied to ancient texts — in this case, those of the Bible — and studies their significance from a historical point of view, but also and above all because it seeks to shed light upon the historical processes which gave rise to biblical texts, diachronic processes that were often complex and involved a long period of time. At the different stages of their production, the texts of the Bible were addressed to various categories of hearers or readers, living in different places and different times.

It is a *critical* method, because in each of its steps (from textual criticism to redaction criticism) it operates with the help of scientific criteria that seek to be as objective as possible. In this way it aims to make accessible to the modern reader the meaning of biblical texts, often very difficult to comprehend.

As an analytical method, it studies the biblical text in the same fashion as it would study any other ancient text and comments upon it as an expression of human discourse. However, above all in the area of redaction criticism, it does allow the exegete, to gain a better grasp of the content of divine revelation.

3. Description

At the present stage of its development, the historical-critical method moves through the following steps:

Textual criticism, as practiced for a very long time, begins the series of scholarly operations. Basing itself on the testimony of the oldest and best manuscripts, as well as of papyri, certain ancient versions and patristic texts, textual-criticism seeks to establish, according to fixed rules, a biblical text as close as possible to the original.

The text is then submitted to a linguistic (morphology and syntax) and semantic analysis, using the knowledge derived from historical philology. It is the role of literary criticism to determine the beginning and end of textual units, large and small, and to establish the internal coherence of the text. The existence of doublets, of irreconcilable differences and of other indicators is a clue to the composite character of certain texts. These can then be divided into small units, the next step being to see whether these in turn can be assigned to different sources. Genre criticism seeks to identify literary genres, the social milieu that give rise to them, their particular features and the history of their development. Tradition criticism situates texts in the stream of tradition and attempts to describe the development of this tradition over the course of time. Finally, redaction criticism studies the modifications that these texts have undergone before being fixed in their final state; it also analyzes this final stage, trying as far as possible to identify the tendencies particularly characteristic of this concluding process. While the preceding steps have sought to explain the text by tracing its origin and development within in a diachronic perspective, this last step concludes with a study that is synchronic: at this point the text is explained as it stands, on the basis of the mutual relationships between its diverse elements, and with an eye to its character as a message communicated by the author to his contemporaries. At this point one is in a position to consider the demands of the text from the point of view of action and life *(fonction pragmatique)*.

When the texts studied belong to a historical literary genre or are related to events of history, historical criticism completes literary criticism, so as to determine the historical significance of the text, in the modern sense of this expression.

It is in this way that one accounts for the various stages that lie behind the biblical revelation in its concrete historical development.

4. Evaluation

What value should we accord to the historical-critical method, especially at this present stage of its development?

It is a method which, when used in an objective manner, implies of itself no *a priori*. If its use is accompanied by *a priori* principles, that is not something pertaining to the method itself, but to certain hermeneutical choices which govern the interpretation and can be tendentious.

Oriented, in its origins, toward source criticism and the history of religions, the method has managed to provide fresh access to the Bible. It has shown the Bible to be a collection of writings, which most often, especially in the case of the Old Testament, are not the creation of a single author, but which have had a long prehistory, inextricably tied either to the history of Israel or to that of the early Church. Previously, the Jewish or Christian interpretation of the Bible had no clear awareness of the concrete and diverse historical conditions in which the Word of God took root among the people; of all this it had only a general and remote awareness. The early confrontation between traditional exegesis and the scientific approach, which initially consciously separated itself from faith and at times even opposed it, was assuredly painful; later however it proved to be salutary: once the method was freed from external prejudices, it led to a more precise understanding of the truth of Sacred Scripture (cf *Dei Verbum*, 12). According to *Divino Afflante Spiritu*, the search for the *literal sense* of Scripture is an essential task of exegesis and, in order to fulfill this task, it is necessary to determine the literary genre of texts (cf *Ench. Bibl.*, 560), something which the historical-critical method helps to achieve.

To be sure, the classic use of the historical-critical method reveals its limitations. It restricts itself to a search for the meaning of the biblical text within the historical circumstances that gave rise to it and is not concerned with other possibilities of meaning which have been revealed at later stages of the biblical revelation and history of the Church. Nonetheless, this method has contributed to the production of works of exegesis and of biblical theology which are of great value.

For a long time now scholars have ceased combining the method with a philosophical system. More recently, there has been a tendency among exegetes to move the method in the direction of a greater insistence upon the form of a text, with less attention paid to its content. But this tendency has been corrected through the application of a more diversified semantics (the semantics of words, phrases, text) and through the study of the demands of the text from the point of view of action and life (*aspect pragmatique*).

With respect to the inclusion, in the method, of a synchronic analysis of texts, we must recognize that we are dealing here with a legitimate operation, for it is the text in its final stage, rather than in its earlier editions, which is the expression of the

Word of God. But diachronic study remains indispensable for making known the historical dynamism which animates Sacred Scripture and for shedding light upon its rich complexity: for example, the Covenant Code (*Exodus* 21-23) reflects a political, social and religious situation of Israelite society different from that reflected in the other law codes preserved in *Deuteronomy* (chapters 12-26) and in *Leviticus* (the Holiness Code, chapters 17-26). We must take care not to replace the historicizing tendency, for which the older historical-critical exegesis is open to criticism, with the opposite excess, that of neglecting history in favor of an exegesis which would be exclusively synchronic.

To sum up, the goal of the historical-critical method is to determine, particularly in a diachronic manner, the meaning expressed by the biblical authors and editors. Along with other methods and approaches, the historical-critical method opens up to the modern reader a path to the meaning of the biblical text, such as we have it today.

B. New Methods of Literary Analysis

No scientific method for the study of the Bible is fully adequate to comprehend the biblical texts in all their richness. For all its overall validity, the historical-critical method cannot claim to be totally sufficient in this respect. It necessarily has to leave aside many aspects of the writings which it studies. It is not surprising, then, that at the present time, other methods and approaches are proposed which serve to explore more profoundly other aspects worthy of attention.

In this section B, we will present certain methods of literary analysis which have been developed recently. In the following sections (C, D, E), we will examine briefly different approaches, some of which relate to the study of the tradition, others to the "human sciences," others still to particular situations of the present time. Finally (F) we will consider the fundamentalist reading of the Bible, a reading which does not accept any systematic approach to interpretation.

Taking advantage of the progress made in our day by linguistic and literary studies, biblical exegesis makes use more and more of new methods of literary analysis, in particular rhetorical analysis, narrative analysis and semiotic analysis.

1. Rhetorical Analysis

Rhetorical analysis in itself is not, in fact, a new method. What is new is the use of it in a systematic way for the interpretation of the Bible and also the start and development of a "new rhetoric."

Rhetoric is the art of composing discourse aimed at persuasion. The fact that all biblical texts are in some measure persuasive in character means that some knowledge of rhetoric should be part of the normal scholarly equipment of all exegetes. Rhetorical analysis must be carried out in a critical way, since scientific exegesis is an undertaking which necessarily submits itself to the demands of the critical mind.

A considerable number of recent studies in the biblical area have devoted considerable attention to the presence of rhetorical features in Scripture. Three different approaches can be distinguished. The first is based upon classical Greco-Roman rhetoric; the second devotes itself to Semitic procedures of composition; the third takes its inspiration from more recent studies — namely, from what is called the "new rhetoric."

Every situation of discourse involves the presence of three elements: the speaker (or author), the discourse (or text) and the audience (or the addressees). *Classical rhetoric* distinguished, accordingly, three factors which contribute to the quality of a discourse as an instrument of persuasion: the authority of the speaker, the force of the argument and the feelings aroused in the audience. The diversity of situation and of audience largely determines the way of speaking adopted. Classical rhetoric, since Aristotle, distinguishes three modes of public speaking: the judicial mode (adopted in a court of law); the deliberative mode (for the political assembly) and the demonstrative mode (for celebratory occasions).

Recognizing the immense influence of rhetoric in Hellenistic culture, a growing number of exegetes make use of treatises on classical rhetoric as an aid toward analyzing certain aspects of biblical texts, especially those of the New Testament.

Other exegetes concentrate upon the characteristic features of the *biblical literary tradition*. Rooted in Semitic culture, this displays a distinct preference for symmetrical compositions, through which one can detect relationships between different elements in the text. The study of the multiple forms of parallelism and other procedures characteristic of the Semitic mode of composition allows for a better discernment of the literary structure of texts, which can only lead to a more adequate understanding of their message.

The "new rhetoric" adopts a more general point of view. It aims to be something more than a simple catalogue of stylistic figures, oratorical stratagems and various kinds of discourse. It investigates what makes a particular use of language effective and successful in the communication of conviction. It seeks to be "realistic" in the sense of not wanting to limit itself to an analysis that is purely formal. It takes due account of the actual situation of debate or discussion. It studies style and composition as means of acting upon an audience. To this end, it benefits from contributions made of late in other areas of knowledge, such as linguistics, semiotics, anthropology and sociology.

Applied to the Bible, the "new rhetoric" aims to penetrate to the very core of the language of revelation precisely as persuasive religious discourse and to measure the impact of such discourse in the social context of the communication thus begun.

Because of the enrichment it brings to the critical study of texts, such rhetorical analysis is worthy of high regard, above all in view of the greater depth achieved in more recent work. It makes up for a negligence of long standing and can lead to the rediscovery or clarification of original perspectives that had been lost or obscured.

The "new rhetoric" is surely right in its drawing attention to the capacity of language to persuade and convince. The Bible is not simply a statement of truths. It is a message that carries within itself a function of communication within a particular context, a message which carries with it a certain power of argument and a rhetorical strategy.

Rhetorical analysis does have, however, limitations. When it remains simply on the level of description, its results often reflect a concern for style only. Basically synchronic in nature, it cannot claim to be an independent method which would be sufficient by itself. Its application to biblical texts raises several questions. Did the authors of these texts belong to the more educated levels of society? To what extent did they follow the rules of rhetoric in their work of composition? What kind of rhetoric is relevant for the analysis of any given text; Greco-Roman or Semitic? Is there sometimes the risk of attributing to certain biblical texts a rhetorical structure that is really too sophisticated? These questions—and there are others—ought not in any way cast doubt upon the use of this kind of analysis; they simply suggest that it is not something to which recourse ought be had without some measure of discernment.

2. Narrative Analysis

Narrative exegesis offers a method of understanding and communicating the biblical message which corresponds to the form of story and personal testimony, something characteristic of Holy Scripture and, of course, a fundamental modality of communication between human persons. The Old Testament in fact presents a story of salvation, the powerful recital of which provides the substance of the profession of faith, liturgy and catechesis (cf *Ps* 78:3-4; *Exod* 12:24-27; *Deut* 6:20-25; 26:5-11). For its own part, the proclamation of the Christian kerygma amounts in essentials to a sequence telling the story of the life, death and resurrection of Jesus Christ, events of which the gospels offer us a detailed account. Catechesis itself also appears in narrative form (cf *1 Cor* 11:23-25).

With respect to the narrative approach, it helps to distinguish methods of analysis, on the one hand, and theological reflection, on the other.

Many *analytic methods* are in fact proposed today. Some start from the study of ancient models of narrative. Others base themselves upon present day "narratology" in one or other of its forms, in which case there can often be points of contact with semiotics. Particularly attentive to elements in the text which have to do with plot, characterization and the point of view taken by a narrator, narrative analysis studies how a text tells a story in such a way as to engage the reader in its "narrative world" and the system of values contained therein.

Several methods introduce a distinction between "real author" and "implied author," "real reader" and "implied reader." The "real author" is the person who actually composed the story. By "implied author" one means the image of the author which the text progressively creates in the course of the reading (with his or her own culture, character, inclinations, faith, etc.). The "real reader" is any person who has access to the text-from those who first read it or heard it read, right down to those who read or hear it today. By "implied reader" one means the reader which the text presupposes and in effect creates, the one who is capable of performing the mental and affective operations necessary for entering into the narrative world of the text and responding to it in the way envisaged by the real author through the instrumentality of the implied author.

A text will continue to have an influence in the degree to which real readers (e.g., ourselves in the late 20th century) can identify with the implied reader. One of the major tasks of exegesis is to facilitate this process of identification.

Narrative analysis involves a new way of understanding how a text works. While the historical-critical method considers the text as a "window" giving access to one or other period (not only to the situation which the story relates but also to that of the community for whom the story is told), narrative analysis insists that the text also functions as a "mirror," in the sense that it projects a certain image — a "narrative world" — which exercises an influence upon readers perceptions in such a way as to bring them to adopt certain values rather than others.

Connected with this kind of study, primarily literary in character, is a certain mode of *theological reflection,* as one considers the implications the "story" (and also the "witness") character of Scripture has with respect to the consent of faith and as one derives from this a hermeneutic of a more practical and pastoral nature. There is here a reaction against the reduction of the inspired text to a series of theological theses, often formulated in non-scriptural categories and language. What is asked of narrative exegesis is that it rehabilitate in new historical contexts the modes of communicating and conveying meaning proper to the biblical account, in order to open up more effectively its saving power. Narrative analysis insists upon the need both to tell the story of salvation (the "informative" aspect) and to tell the story in view of salvation (the "performative" aspect). The biblical account, in effect, whether explicitly or implicitly as the case may be, contains an existential appeal addressed to the reader.

The usefulness of narrative analysis for the exegesis of the Bible is clear. It is well suited to the narrative character which so many biblical texts display. It can facilitate the transition, often so difficult, from the meaning of the text in its historical context (the proper object of the historical-critical method) to its significance for the reader of today. On the other hand, the distinction between the "real author" and the "implied author" does tend to make problems of interpretation somewhat more complex.

When applied to texts of the Bible, narrative analysis cannot rest content with imposing upon them certain pre-established models. It must strive to adapt itself to their own proper character. The synchronic approach which it brings to texts needs to be supplemented by diachronic studies as well. It must, moreover, beware of a tendency that can arise to exclude any kind of doctrinal elaboration in the content of biblical narratives. In such a case it would find itself out of step with the biblical tradition itself, which practices precisely this kind of elaboration, and also with the tradition of the Church, which has continued further along the same way. Finally, it is worth noting that the existential subjective effectiveness of the impact of the Word of God in its narrative transmission cannot be considered to be in itself a sufficient indication that its full truth has been adequately grasped.

3. *Semiotic Analysis*

Ranged among the methods identified as synchronic, those, namely, which concentrate on the study of the biblical text as it comes before the reader in its final state, is semiotic analysis. This has experienced a notable development in certain quarters over the last twenty years. Originally known by the more general term "structuralism," this method can claim as forefather the Swiss linguist Ferdinand de Saussure, who at the beginning of the present century worked out the theory according to which all language is a system of relationships obeying fixed laws. Several linguists and literary critics have had a notable influence in the development of the method. The majority of biblical scholars who make use of semiotics in the study of the Bible take as their authority Algirdas J. Greimas and the School of Paris which he founded. Similar approaches and methods, based upon modern linguistics, have developed elsewhere. But it is Greimas' method which we intend to present and analyze briefly here.

Semiotics is based upon three main principles or presuppositions:

The *principle of immanence:* each text forms a unit of meaning complete in itself; the analysis considers the entire text but only the text; it does not look to any date "external" to the text, such as the author, the audience, any events it describes or what might have been its process of composition.

The *principle of the structure of meaning:* there is no meaning given except in and through relationship, in particular the relationship of "difference"; the analysis of the text consists then in establishing the network of relationships (of opposition, confirmation, etc.) between the various elements; out of this the meaning of the text is constructed.

The *principle of the grammar of the text:* each text follows a "grammar," that is to say, a certain number of rules or structures; in the collection of sentences that we call discourse there are various levels, each of which has its own distinct grammar.

The overall content of a text can be analyzed at three different levels.

The narrative level. Here one studies in the story the transformations which move the action from the initial to the final state. Within the course of the narrative, the analysis seeks to retrace the different phases, logically bound to each other, which mark the transformation from one state to another. In each of these phases it establishes the relationships between the "roles" played by the "actants" which determine the various stages of development and bring about transformation.

The level of discourse. The analysis here consists of three operations: (a) the fixing and classification of figures, that is to say, the elements of meaning in a text (actors, times, places); (b) the tracking of the course of each figure in the text in order to determine just how the text uses each one; (c) inquiry into the thematic value of the figures. This last operation consists in discerning "in the name of what" (= what value) the figures follow such a path in the text determined in this way.

The logico-semantic level. This is the so-called deep level. It is also the most abstract. It proceeds from the assumption that certain forms of logic and meaning underlie the narrative and discursive organization of all discourse. The analysis at this level consists in identifying the logic which governs the basic articulations of the narrative and figurative flow of a text. To achieve this, recourse is often had to an instrument called the "semiotic square" (*carré sémiotique),* a figure which makes use of the relationships between two "contrary" terms and two "contradictory" terms (for example, black and white; white and not-white; black and not-black).

The exponents of the theory behind the semiotic method continue to produce new developments. Present research centers most particularly upon enunciation and intertextuality. Applied in the first instance to the narrative texts of Scripture, to which it is most readily applicable, the use of the method has been more and more extended to other kinds of biblical discourse as well.

The description of semiotics that has been given and above all the formulation of its presuppositions should have already served to make clear the *advantages* and the *limitations* of this method. By directing greater attention to the fact that each biblical text is a coherent whole, obedient to a precise linguistic mechanic of operation, semiotics contributes to our understanding of the Bible as Word of God expressed in human language.

Semiotics can be usefully employed in the study of the Bible only in so far as the method is separated from certain assumptions developed in structuralist philosophy, namely the refusal to accept individual personal identity within the text and extra-textual reference beyond it. The Bible is a Word that bears upon reality, a Word which God has spoken in a historical context and which God addresses to us today through the mediation of human authors. The semiotic approach must be open to history: first of all to the history of those who play a part in the texts; then to that of the authors and readers. The great risk run by those who employ semiotic analysis is that of remaining at the level of a formal study of the content of texts, failing to draw out the message.

When it does not become lost in remote and complex language and when its principle elements are taught in simple terms, semiotic analysis can give Christians a taste for studying the biblical text and discovering certain of its dimensions, without their first having to acquire a great deal of instruction in historical matters relating to the production of the text and its socio-cultural world. It can thus prove useful in pastoral practice itself, providing a certain appropriation of Scripture among those who are not specialized in the area.

C. Approaches Based on Tradition

The literary methods which we have just reviewed, although they differ from the historical-critical method in that they pay greater attention to the internal unity of the texts studied, remain nonetheless insufficient for the interpretation of the Bible, because they consider each of its writings in isolation. But the Bible is not a compilation of texts unrelated to each other; rather, it is a gathering together of a whole array of witnesses from one great Tradition. To be fully adequate to the object of its study, biblical exegesis must keep this truth firmly in mind. Such in fact is the perspective adopted by a number of approaches which are being developed at present.

1. *The Canonical Approach*

The "canonical" approach, which originated in the United States some twenty years ago, proceeds from the perception that the historical-critical method experiences at times considerable difficulty in arriving, in its conclusions, at a truly theological level. It aims to carry out the theological task of interpretation more successfully by beginning from within an explicit framework of faith: the Bible as a whole.

To achieve this, it interprets each biblical text in the light of the Canon of Scriptures, that is to say, of the Bible as received as the norm of faith by a community of believers. It seeks to situate each text within the single plan of God, the goal being to arrive at a presentation of Scripture truly valid for our time. The method does not claim to be a substitute for the historical-critical method; the hope is, rather, to complete it.

Two different points of view have been proposed:

Brevard S. Childs centers his interest on the final canonical form of the text (whether book or collection), the form accepted by the community as an authoritative expression of its faith and rule of life.

James A. Sanders, rather than looking to the final and fixed form of the text, devotes his attention to the "canonical process" or progressive development of the Scriptures which the believing community has accepted as a normative authority. The critical study of this process examines the way in which older traditions have been used again and again in new contexts, before finally coming to constitute a whole that is at once stable and yet adaptable, coherent while holding together matter that is diverse — in short, a complete whole, in which the faith community can find its identity. In the course of this process various hermeneutic procedures have been at work and this continues to be the case even after the fixing of the canon. These procedures are often midrashic in nature, serving to make the biblical text relevant for a later time. They encourage a constant interaction between the community and the Scriptures, calling for an interpretation which ever seeks to bring the tradition up to date.

The canonical approach rightly reacts against placing an exaggerated value upon what is supposed to be original and early, as if this alone were authentic. Inspired Scripture is precisely Scripture in that it has been recognized by the Church as the rule of faith. Hence the significance, in this light, of both the final form in which each of the books of the Bible appears and of the complete whole which all together make up as Canon. Each individual book only becomes biblical in the light of the Canon as a whole.

It is the believing community that provides a truly adequate context for interpreting canonical texts. In this context faith and the Holy Spirit enrich exegesis; Church authority, exercised as a service of the community, must see to it that this interpretation remains faithful to the great Tradition which has produced the texts (cf *Dei Verbum,* 10).

The canonical approach finds itself grappling with more than one problem when it seeks to define the "canonical process." At what point in time precisely does a text become canonical? It seems reasonable to describe it as such from the time that the community attributes to it a normative authority, even if this should be before it has reached its final, definitive form. One can speak of a "canonical" hermeneutic once the repetition of the traditions, which comes about through the taking into account of new aspects of the situation (be they religious, cultural or theological), begins to preserve the identity of the message. But a question arises: should the interpretive process which led to the formation of the Canon be recognized as the guiding principle for the interpretation of Scripture today?

On the other hand, the complex relationships that exist between the Jewish and Christian Canons of Scripture raise many problems of interpretation. The Christian Church has received as "Old Testament" the writings which had authority in the Hellenistic Jewish community, but some of these are either lacking in the Hebrew Bible or appear there in somewhat different form. The *corpus* is therefore different. From this it follows that the canonical interpretation cannot be identical in each case, granted that each text must be read in relation to the whole *corpus.* But, above all, the Church reads the Old Testament in the light of the paschal mystery — the death and resurrection of Jesus Christ — who brings a radical newness and, with sovereign authority, gives a meaning to the Scriptures that is decisive and definitive (cf *Dei Verbum,* 4). This new determination of meaning has become an integral element of

Christian faith. It ought not, however, mean doing away with all attempt to be consistent with that earlier canonical interpretation which preceded the Christian Passover. One must respect each stage of the history of salvation. To empty out of the Old Testament its own proper meaning would be to deprive the New of its roots in history.

2. Approach through Recourse to Jewish Traditions of Interpretation

The Old Testament reached its final form in the Jewish world of the four or five centuries preceding the Christian era. Judaism of this time also provided the matrix for the origin of the New Testament and the infant Church. Numerous studies of the history of ancient Judaism and notably the manifold research stimulated by the discoveries at Qumran have highlighted the complexity of the Jewish world, both in the land of Israel and in the Diaspora, throughout this period.

It is in this world that the interpretation of Scripture had its beginning. One of the most ancient witnesses to the Jewish interpretation of the Bible is the Greek translation known as the Septuagint. The Aramaic Targums represent a further witness to the same activity, which has carried on down to the present, giving rise in the process to an immense mass of learned procedures for the preservation of the text of the Old Testament and for the explanation of the meaning of biblical texts. At all stages, the more astute Christian exegetes, from Origen and Jerome onwards, have sought to draw profit from the Jewish biblical learning in order to acquire a better understanding of Scripture. Many modern exegetes follow this example.

The ancient Jewish traditions allow for a better understanding particularly of the Septuagint, the Jewish Bible which eventually became the first part of the Christian Bible for at least the first four centuries of the Church and has remained so in the East down to the present day. The extra-canonical Jewish literature, called apocryphal or intertestamental, in its great abundance and variety, is an important source for the interpretation of the New Testament. The variety of exegetical procedures practiced by the different strains of Judaism can actually be found within the Old Testament itself, for example, in *Chronicles* with reference to the Books of *Samuel* and *Kings*, and also within the New Testament, as for example in certain ways Paul goes about argument from Scripture. A great variety of forms — parables, allegories, anthologies and *florilegia, re-readings (relectures), pesher* technique, methods of associating otherwise unrelated texts, psalms and hymns, vision, revelation and dream sequences, wisdom compositions — all are common to both the Old and the New Testaments, as well as in Jewish circles before and after the time of Jesus. The Targums and the Midrashic literature illustrate the homiletic tradition and mode of biblical interpretation practiced by wide sectors of Judaism in the first centuries.

Many Christian exegetes of the Old Testament look, besides, to the Jewish commentators, grammarians and lexicographers of the medieval and more recent period as a resource for understanding difficult passages or expressions that are either rare or unique. References to such Jewish works appear in current exegetical discussion much more frequently than was formerly the case.

Jewish biblical scholarship in all its richness, from its origins in antiquity down to the present day, is an asset of the highest value for the exegesis of both Testaments, provided that it be used with discretion. Ancient Judaism took many diverse forms. The Pharisaic form which eventually came to be the most prevalent, in the shape of rabbinic Judaism, was by no means the only one. The range of ancient Jewish texts extends across several centuries; it is important to rank them in chronological order before proceeding to make comparisons. Above all, the overall pattern of the Jewish and Christian communities is very different: on the Jewish side, in very varied ways, it is a question of a religion which defines a people and a way of life based upon written revelation and an oral tradition; whereas, on the Christian side, it is faith in the Lord Jesus—the one who died, was raised and lives still, Messiah and Son of God; it is around faith in his person that the community is gathered. These two diverse starting points create, as regards the interpretation of the Scriptures, two separate contexts, which for all their points of contact and similarity, are in fact radically diverse.

3. *Approach by the History of the Influence of the Text (Wirkungsgeschichte)*

This approach rests upon two principles: *a)* a text only becomes a literary work in so far as it encounters readers who give life to it by appropriating it to themselves; *b)* this appropriation of the text, which can occur either on the individual or community level and can take shape in various spheres (literary, artistic, theological, ascetical and mystical), contributes to a better understanding of the text itself.

Without being entirely unknown in antiquity, this approach was developed in literary studies between 1960 and 1970, a time when criticism became interested in the relation between a text and its readers. Biblical studies can only draw profit from research of this kind, all the more so since the philosophy of hermeneutics for its own part stresses the necessary distance between a work and its author, as well as between a work and its readers. Within this perspective, the history of the effect produced by a book or a passage of Scripture *("Wirkungsgeschichte")* begins to enter into the work of interpretation. Such an inquiry seeks to assess the development of interpretation over the course of time under the influence of the concerns readers have brought to the text. It also attempts to evaluate the importance of the role played by tradition in finding meaning in biblical texts.

The mutual presence to each other of text and readers creates its own dynamic, for the text exercises an influence and provokes reactions. It makes a resonant claim, that is heard by readers, whether as individuals or as members of a group. The reader is in any case never an isolated subject. He or she belongs to a social context and lives within a tradition. Readers come to the text with their own questions, exercise a certain selectivity, propose an interpretation and, in the end, are able either to create a further work or else take initiatives inspired directly from their reading of Scripture.

Numerous examples of such an approach are already evident. The history of the reading of the *Song of Songs* offers an excellent illustration: it would show how this book was received in the Patristic period, in monastic circles of the mediaeval Church and then again how it was taken up by a mystical writer such as St. John of the Cross. The approach thus offers a better chance of uncovering all the dimensions of meaning contained in such a writing. Similarly, in the New Testament, it is both possible and useful to throw light upon the meaning of a passage (for example, that of the rich young man in *Matt* 19:16-26) by pointing out how fruitful its influence has been throughout the history of the Church.

At the same time, history also illustrates the prevalence from time to time of interpretations that are tendentious and false, baneful in their effect — such as, for example, those that have promoted antisemitism or other forms of racial discrimination or, yet again, various kinds of millenarian delusions. This serves to show that this approach cannot constitute a discipline that would be purely autonomous. Discernment is required. Care must be exercised not to privilege one or other stage of the history of the text's influence to such an extent that it becomes the sole norm of its interpretation for all time.

D. Approaches that Use the Human Sciences

In order to communicate itself, the Word of God has taken root in the life of human communities (cf *Sir* 24:12) and it has been through the psychological dispositions of the various persons who composed the biblical writings that it has pursued its path. It follows, then, that the human sciences — in particular, sociology, anthropology and psychology — can contribute toward a better understanding of certain aspects of biblical texts. It should be noted, however, that in this area there are several schools of thought, with notable disagreement among them upon the very nature of these sciences. That said, a good number of exegetes have drawn considerable profit in recent years from research of this kind.

1. The Sociological Approach

Religious texts are bound in reciprocal relationship to the societies in which they originate. This is clearly the case as regards biblical texts. Consequently, the scientific study of the Bible requires as exact a knowledge as is possible of the social conditions distinctive of the various milieus in which the traditions recorded in the Bible took shape. This kind of socio-historical information needs then to be completed by an accurate sociological explanation, which will provide a scientific interpretation of the implications for each case of the prevailing social conditions.

The sociological point of view has had a role in the history of exegesis for quite some time. The attention which form-criticism devoted to the social circumstances in which various texts arose *(Sitz im Leben)* is already an indication of this: it recognized that biblical traditions bore the mark of the socio-cultural milieu which transmitted them. In the first third of the 20th century, the Chicago School studied the socio-historical situation of early Christianity, thereby giving historical criticism a notable impulse in this direction. In the course of the last twenty years (1970-1990), the sociological approach to biblical texts has become an integral part of exegesis.

The questions which arise in this area for the exegesis of the Old Testament are manifold. One should ask, for example, concerning the various forms of social and religious organization which Israel has known in the course of its history. For the period before the formation of a nation-state, does the ethnological model of a society which is segmentary and lacking a unifying head (acephalous) provide a satisfactory base from which to work? What has been the process whereby a loosely organized tribal league became, first of all, an organized monarchical state and, after that, a community held together simply by bonds of religion and common descent? What economic, military and other transformations were brought about by the movement toward political and religious centralization that led to the monarchy? Does not the study of the laws regulating social behavior in the ancient Near East and in Israel make a more useful contribution to the understanding of the Decalogue than purely literary attempts to reconstruct the earliest form of the text?

For the exegesis of the New Testament, the questions will clearly be somewhat different. Let us mention some: to account for the way of life adopted by Jesus and his disciples before Easter, what value can be accorded to the theory of a movement of itinerant charismatic figures, living without fixed home, without family, without money and other goods? In the matter of the call to follow in the steps of Jesus, can we speak of a genuine relationship of continuity between the radical detachment involved in following Jesus in his earthly life and what was asked of members of the Christian movement after Easter in the very different social conditions of early Christianity? What do we know of the social structure of the Pauline communities, taking account in each case of the relevant urban culture?

In general, the sociological approach broadens the exegetical enterprise and brings to it many positive aspects. Knowledge of sociological data which help us understand the economic, cultural and religious functioning of the biblical world is indispensable for historical criticism. The task incumbent upon the exegete, to gain a better understanding of the early Church's witness to faith, cannot be achieved in a fully rigorous way without the scientific research which studies the strict relationship that exists between the texts of the New Testament and life as actually lived by the early Church. The employment of models provided by sociological science offers historical studies into the biblical period a notable potential for renewal — though it is necessary, of course, that the models employed be modified in accordance with the reality under study.

Here let us signal some of the risks involved in applying the sociological approach to exegesis. It is surely the case that, if the work of sociology consists in the study of currently existing societies, one can expect difficulty when seeking to apply its methods to historical societies belonging to a very distant past.

Psychological and psychoanalytical studies do bring a certain enrichment to biblical exegesis in that, because of them, the texts of the Bible can be better understood in terms of experience of life and norms of behavior. As is well known, religion is always in a relationship of conflict or debate with the unconscious. It plays a significant role in the proper orientation of human drives. The stages through which historical criticism passes in its methodical study of texts need to be complemented by study of the different levels of reality they display. Psychology and psychoanalysis attempt to show the way in this respect. They lead to a multidimensional understanding of Scripture and help decode the human language of Revelation.

Psychology and, in a somewhat different way, psycho-analysis have led, in particular, to a new understanding of symbol. The language of symbol makes provision for the expression of areas of religious experience that are not accessible to purely conceptual reasoning but which have a genuine value for the expression of truth. For this reason, interdisciplinary study conducted in common by exegetes and psychologists or psychoanalysts offers particular advantages, especially when objectively grounded and confirmed by pastoral experience.

Numerous examples could be cited showing the necessity of a collaborative effort on the part of exegetes and psychologists: to ascertain the meaning of cultic ritual, of sacrifice, of bans, to explain the use of imagery in biblical language, the metaphorical significance of miracle stories, the wellsprings of apocalyptic, visual and auditory experiences. It is not simply a matter of describing the symbolic language of the Bible but of grasping how it functions with respect to the revelation of mystery and the issuing of challenge — where the "numinous" reality of God enters into contact with the human person.

The dialogue between exegesis and psychology or psychoanalysis, begun with a view to a better understanding of the Bible, should clearly be conducted in a critical manner, respecting the boundaries of each discipline. Whatever the circumstances, a psychology or psychoanalysis of an atheistic nature disqualifies itself from giving proper consideration to the data of faith. Useful as they may be to determine more exactly the extent of human responsibility, psychology and psychoanalysis should not serve to eliminate the reality of sin and of salvation. One should, moreover, take care not to confuse spontaneous religiosity and biblical revelation or impugn the historical character of the Bible's message, which bestows upon it the value of a unique event.

Let us note moreover that one cannot speak of "psychoanalytical exegesis" as though it existed in one single form. In fact, proceeding from the different fields of psychology and from the various schools of thought, there exists a whole range of approaches capable of shedding helpful light upon the human and theological interpretation of the Bible. To absolutize one or other of the approaches taken by the various schools of psychology and psychoanalysis would not serve to make collaborative effort in this area more fruitful but rather render it harmful.

The human sciences are not confined to sociology, cultural anthropology and psychology. Other disciplines can also be very useful for the interpretation of the Bible. In all these areas, it is necessary to take good account of competence in the particular field and to recognize that only rarely will one and the same person be fully qualified in both exegesis and one or other of the human sciences.

E. Contextual Approaches

The interpretation of a text is always dependent on the mindset and concerns of its readers. Readers give privileged attention to certain aspects and, without even being aware of it, neglect others. Thus it is inevitable that some exegetes bring to their work points of view that are new and responsive to contemporary currents of thought which have not up till now been taken sufficiently into consideration. It is important that they do so with critical discernment. The movements in this regard which claim particular attention today are those of liberation theology and feminism.

1. The Liberationist Approach

The theology of liberation is a complex phenomenon, which ought not be oversimplified. It began to establish itself as a theological movement in the early 1970s. Over and beyond the economic, social and political circumstances of Latin America, its starting point is to be found in two great events in the recent life of the Church: the Second Vatican Council, with its declared intention of *aggiornamento* and of orienting the pastoral work of the Church toward the needs of the contemporary world, and the Second General Conference of the Episcopate of Latin America held at Medelin in 1968, which applied the teachings of the Council to the needs of Latin America. The movement has since spread also to other parts of the world (Africa, Asia, the black population of the United States).

It is not all that easy to discern if there truly exists "one" theology of liberation and to define what its methodology might be. It is equally difficult to determine adequately its manner of reading the Bible, in a way which would lead to an accurate assessment of advantages and limitations. One can say that liberation theology adopts no particular methodology. But, starting from its own socio-cultural and political point of view, it practices a reading of the Bible which is oriented to the needs of the people, who seek in the Scriptures nourishment for their faith and their life.

Liberation theology is not content with an objectifying interpretation which concentrates on what the text said in its original context. It seeks a reading drawn from the situation of people as it is lived here and now. If a people lives in circumstances of oppression, one must go to the Bible to find there nourishment capable of sustaining the people in its struggles and its hopes. The reality of the present time should not be ignored but, on the contrary, met head on, with a view to shedding upon it the light of the Word. From this light will come authentic Christian praxis, leading to the transformation of society through works of justice and love. Within the vision of faith, Scripture is transformed into a dynamic impulse for full liberation.

The main *principles* guiding this approach are the following:

God is present in the history of his people, bringing them salvation. He is the God of the poor and cannot tolerate oppression or injustice.

It follows that exegesis cannot be neutral, but must, in imitation of God, take sides on behalf of the poor and be engaged in the struggle to liberate the oppressed.

It is precisely participation in this struggle that allows those interpretations to surface which are discovered only when the biblical texts are read in a context of solidarity with the oppressed.

Because the liberation of the oppressed is a communal process, the community of the poor is the privileged addressee of the Bible as word of liberation. Moreover, since the biblical

various periods. It pays no attention to the literary forms and to the human ways of thinking to be found in the biblical texts, many of which are the result of a process extending over long periods of time and bearing the mark of very diverse historical situations.

Fundamentalism also places undue stress upon the inerrancy of certain details in the biblical texts, especially in what concerns historical events or supposedly scientific truth. It often historicizes material which from the start never claimed to be historical. It considers historical everything that is reported or recounted with verbs in the past tense, failing to take the necessary account of the possibility of symbolic or figurative meaning.

Fundamentalism often shows a tendency to ignore or to deny the problems presented by the biblical text in its original Hebrew, Aramaic or Greek form. It is often narrowly bound to one fixed translation, whether old or present-day. By the same token, it fails to take account of the "re-readings" (relectures) of certain texts which are found within the Bible itself.

In what concerns the Gospels, fundamentalism does not take into account the development of the gospel tradition, but naively confuses the final stage of this tradition (what the evangelists have written) with the initial (the words and deeds of the historical Jesus). At the same time fundamentalism neglects an important fact: the way in which the first Christian communities themselves understood the impact produced by Jesus of Nazareth and his message. But it is precisely there that we find a witness to the apostolic origin of the Christian faith and its direct expression. Fundamentalism thus misrepresents the call voiced by the gospel itself.

Fundamentalism likewise tends to adopt very narrow points of view. It accepts the literal reality of an ancient, out-of-date cosmology, simply because it is found expressed in the Bible;

this blocks any dialogue with a broader way of seeing the relationship between culture and faith. Its relying upon a non-critical reading of certain texts of the Bible serves to reinforce political ideas and social attitudes that are marked by prejudices — racism, for example — quite contrary to the Christian gospel.

Finally, in its attachment to the principle "Scripture alone," fundamentalism separates the interpretation of the Bible from the Tradition, which, guided by the Spirit, has authentically developed in union with Scripture in the heart of the community of faith. It fails to realize that the New Testament took form within the Christian Church and that it is the Holy Scripture of this Church, the existence of which preceded the composition of the texts. Because of this, fundamentalism is often anti-Church; it considers of little importance the creeds, the doctrines and liturgical practices which have become part of Church tradition, as well as the teaching function of the Church itself. It presents itself as a form of private interpretation which does not acknowledge that the Church is founded on the Bible and draws its life and inspiration from Scripture.

The fundamentalist approach is dangerous, for it is attractive to people who look to the Bible for ready answers to the problems of life. It can deceive these people, offering them interpretations that are pious but illusory, instead of telling them that the Bible does not necessarily contain an immediate answer to each and every problem. Without saying as much in so many words, fundamentalism actually invites people to a kind of intellectual suicide. It injects into life a false certitude, for it unwittingly confuses the divine substance of the biblical message with what are in fact its human limitations.

II. Hermeneutical Questions

A. Philosophical Hermeneutics

In its recent course exegesis has been challenged to some rethinking in the light of contemporary philosophical hermeneutics, which has stressed the involvement of the knowing subject in human understanding, especially as regards historical knowledge. Hermeneutical reflection took new life with the publication of the works of Friedrich Schleiermacher, Wilhelm Dilthey and, above all, Martin Heidegger. In the footsteps of these philosophers, but also to some extent moving away from them, various authors have more deeply developed contemporary hermeneutical theory and its applications to Scripture. Among them we will mention especially Rudolf Bultmann, Hans Georg Gadamer and Paul Ricoeur. It is not possible to give a complete summary of their thought here. It will be enough to indicate certain central ideas of their philosophies which have had their impact on the interpretation of biblical texts.[3]

1. Modern Perspectives

Conscious of the cultural distance between the world of the 1st century and that of the 20th, Bultmann was particularly anxious to make the reality of which the Bible treats speak to his contemporaries. He insisted upon the "pre-understanding" necessary for all understanding and elaborated the theory of the

---

3. The hermeneutic of the Word developed by Gerhard Ebeling and Ernst Fuchs adopts a different approach and proceeds from another field of thought. It involves more a theological rather than a philosophical hermeneutic. Ebeling agrees however with such authors as Bultmann and Ricoeur in affirming that the Word of God finds its true meaning only in the encounter with those to whom it is addressed.

existential interpretation of the New Testament writings. Relying upon the thinking of Heidegger, Bultmann insisted that it is not possible to have an exegesis of a biblical text without presuppositions which guide comprehension. "Pre-understanding" *("Vorverständnis")* is founded upon the life-relationship *("Lebensverhältnis")* of the interpreter to the reality of which the text speaks. To avoid subjectivism, however, one must allow preunderstanding to be deepened and enriched — even to be modified and corrected — by the reality of the text.

Bultmann asked what might be the most appropriate frame of thought for defining the sort of questions that would render the texts of Scripture understandable to people of today. He claimed to have found the answer in the existential analysis of Heidegger, maintaining that Heideggerian existential principles have a universal application and offer structures and concepts most appropriate for the understanding of human existence as revealed in the New Testament message.

Gadamer likewise stresses the historical distance between the text and its interpreter. He takes up and develops the theory of the hermeneutical circle. Anticipations and preconceptions affecting our understanding stem from the tradition which carries us. This tradition consists in a mass of historical and cultural data which constitute our life context and our horizon of understanding. The interpreter is obliged to enter into dialogue with the reality at stake in the text. Understanding is reached in the fusion of the differing horizons of text and reader *("Horizontverschmelzung")*. This is possible only to the extent that there is a "belonging" *("Zugehörigkeit"),* that is, a fundamental affinity, between the interpreter and his or her object. Hermeneutics is a dialectical process: the understanding of a text always entails an enhanced understanding of oneself.

With regard to the hermeneutical thought of Ricoeur, the principal thing to note is the highlighting of the function of distantiation. This is the necessary prelude to any correct appropriation of a text. A first distancing occurs between the text and its author, for, once produced, the text takes on a certain autonomy in relation to its author; it begins its own career of meaning. Another distancing exists between the text and its successive readers; these have to respect the world of the text in its otherness. Thus the methods of literary and historical analysis are necessary for interpretation. Yet the meaning of a text can be fully grasped only as it is actualized in the lives of readers who appropriate it. Beginning with their situation, they are summoned to uncover new meanings, along the fundamental line of meaning indicated by the text. Biblical knowledge should not stop short at language; it must seek to arrive at the reality of which the language speaks. The religious language of the Bible is a symbolic language which "gives rise to thought" *("donne à penser"),* a language the full richness of which one never ceases to discover, a language which points to a transcendent reality and which, at the same time, awakens human beings to the deepest dimensions of personal existence.

2. Usefulness for Exegesis

What is to be said about these contemporary theories of the interpretation of texts? The Bible is the Word of God for all succeeding ages. Hence the absolute necessity of a hermeneutical theory which allows for the incorporation of the methods of literary and historical criticism within a broader model of interpretation. It is a question of overcoming the distance between the time of the authors and first addressees of the biblical texts and our own contemporary age, and of doing so in a way that permits a correct actualization of the scriptural message so that the Christian life of faith may find nourishment. All exegesis of texts is thus summoned to make itself fully complete through a "hermeneutics" understood in this modern sense.

The Bible itself and the history of its interpretation point to the need for a hermeneutics — for an interpretation, that is, that proceeds from and addresses our world today. The whole complex of the Old and New Testament writings show themselves to be the product of a long process where founding events constantly find reinterpretation through connection with the life of communities of faith. In Church tradition, the Fathers, as first interpreters of Scripture, considered that their exegesis of texts was complete only when it had found a meaning relevant to the situation of Christians in their own day. Exegesis is truly faithful to proper intention of biblical texts when it goes not only to the heart of their formulation to find the reality of faith there expressed but also seeks to link this reality to the experience of faith in our present world.

Contemporary hermeneutics is a healthy reaction to historical positivism and to the temptation to apply to the study of the Bible the purely objective criteria used in the natural sciences. On the one hand, all events reported in the Bible are interpreted events. On the other, all exegesis of the accounts of these events necessarily involves the exegete's own subjectivity. Access to a proper understanding of biblical texts is only granted to the person who has an affinity with what the text is saying on the basis of life experience. The question which faces every exegete is this: which hermeneutical theory best enables a proper grasp of the profound reality of which Scripture speaks and its meaningful expression for people today?

We must frankly accept that certain hermeneutical theories

are inadequate for interpreting Scripture. For example, Bultmann's existentialist interpretation tends to enclose the Christian message within the constraints of a particular philosophy. Moreover, by virtue of the presuppositions insisted upon in this hermeneutic, the religious message of the Bible is for the most part emptied of its objective reality (by means of an excessive "demythologization") and tends to be reduced to an anthropological message only. Philosophy becomes the norm of interpretation, rather than an instrument for understanding the central object of all interpretation: the person of Jesus Christ and the saving events accomplished in human history. An authentic interpretation of Scripture, then, involves in the first place a welcoming of the meaning that is given in the events and, in a supreme way, in the person of Jesus Christ.

This meaning is expressed in the text. To avoid, then, purely subjective readings, an interpretation valid for contemporary times will be founded on the study of the text and such an interpretation will constantly submit its presuppositions to verification by the text.

Biblical hermeneutics, for all that it is a part of the general hermeneutics applying to every literary and historical text, constitutes at the same time a unique instance of general hermeneutics. Its specific characteristics stem from its object. The events of salvation and their accomplishment in the person of Jesus Christ give meaning to all human history. New interpretations in the course of time can only be the unveiling or unfolding of this wealth of meaning. Reason alone cannot fully comprehend the account of these events given in the Bible. Particular presuppositions, such as the faith lived in ecclesial community and the light of the Spirit, control its interpretation. As the reader matures in the life of the Spirit, so there grows also his or her capacity to understand the realities of which the Bible speaks.

B. The Meaning of Inspired Scripture

The contribution made by modern philosophical hermeneutics and the recent development of literary theory allows biblical exegesis to deepen its understanding of the task before it, the complexity of which has become ever more evident. Ancient exegesis, which obviously could not take into account modern scientific requirements, attributed to every text of Scripture several levels of meaning. The most prevalent distinction was that between the literal sense and the spiritual sense. Medieval exegesis distinguished within the spiritual sense three different aspects, each relating, respectively, to the truth revealed, to the way of life commended and to the final goal to be achieved. From this came the famous couplet of Augustine of Denmark (13th century):

> *"Littera gesta docet, quid credas allegoria,*
> *moralis quid agas, quid speras anagogia."*

In reaction to this multiplicity of senses, historical-critical exegesis adopted, more or less overtly, the thesis of the one single meaning: a text cannot have at the same time more than one meaning. All the effort of historical-critical exegesis goes into defining "the" precise sense of this or that biblical text seen within the circumstances in which it was produced.

But this thesis has now run aground on the conclusions of theories of language and of philosophical hermeneutics, both of which affirm that written texts are open to a plurality of meaning.

The problem is not simple and it arises in different ways in regard to different types of texts: historical accounts, parables, oracular pronouncements, laws, proverbs, prayers, hymns, etc. Nevertheless, while keeping in mind that considerable diversity of opinion also prevails, some general principles can be stated.

1. The Literal Sense

It is not only legitimate, it is also absolutely necessary to seek to define the precise meaning of texts as produced by their authors—what is called the "literal" meaning. St. Thomas Aquinas had already affirmed the fundamental importance of this sense (*S. Th.* I, q. 1, a. 10, ad 1).

The literal sense is not to be confused with the "literalist" sense to which fundamentalists are attached. It is not sufficient to translate a text word for word in order to obtain its literal sense. One must understand the text according to the literary conventions of the time. When a text is metaphorical, its literal sense is not that which flows immediately from a word to word translation (e.g., "Let your loins be girt": *Luke* 12:35), but that which corresponds to the metaphorical use of these terms ("Be ready for action"). When it is a question of a story, the literal sense does not necessarily imply belief that the facts recounted actually took place, for a story need not belong to the genre of history but be instead a work of imaginative fiction.

The literal sense of Scripture is that which has been expressed directly by the inspired human authors. Since it is the fruit of inspiration, this sense is also intended by God, as principal author. One arrives at this sense by means of a careful analysis of the text, within its literary and historical context. The principal task of exegesis is to carry out this analysis, making use of all the resources of literary and historical research, with a view to defining the literal sense of the biblical texts with the greatest possible accuracy (cf *Divino Afflante Spiritu: EB* 550). To this end, the study of ancient literary genres is particularly necessary (*ibid.* 560).

Does a text have only one literal sense? In general, yes; but there is no question here of a hard and fast rule, and this for two reasons. First, a human author can intend to refer at one and the same time to more than one level of reality. This is in fact normally the case with regard to poetry. Biblical inspiration does not reject this capacity of human psychology and language; the fourth Gospel offers numerous examples of it. Secondly, even when a human utterance appears to have only one meaning, divine inspiration can guide the expression in such way as to create more than one meaning. This is the case with the saying of Caiaphas in *John* 11:50: at one and the same time it expresses both an immoral political ploy and a divine revelation. The two aspects belong, both of them, to the literal sense, for they are both made clear by the context. Although this example may be extreme, it remains significant, providing a warning against adopting too narrow a conception of the inspired text's literal sense.

One should be especially attentive to the *dynamic aspect* of many texts. The meaning of the royal psalms, for example, should not be limited strictly to the historical circumstances of their production. In speaking of the king, the psalmist evokes at one and the same time both the institution as it actually was and an idealized vision of kingship as God intended it to be; in this way the text carries the reader beyond the institution of kingship in its actual historical manifestation. Historical-critical exegesis has too often tended to limit the meaning of texts by tying it too rigidly to precise historical circumstances. It should seek rather to determine the direction of thought expressed by the text; this direction, far from working toward a limitation of meaning, will on the contrary dispose the exegete to perceive extensions of it that are more or less foreseeable in advance.

One branch of modern hermeneutics has stressed that human speech gains an altogether fresh status when put in writing. A written text has the capacity to be placed in new circumstances, which will illuminate it in different ways, adding new meanings to the original sense. This capacity of written texts is especially operative in the case of the biblical writings, recognized as the Word of God. Indeed, what encouraged the believing community to preserve these texts was the conviction that they would continue to be bearers of light and life for generations of believers to come. The literal sense is, from the start, open to further developments, which are produced through the "re-reading" ("relectures") of texts in new contexts.

It does not follow from this that we can attribute to a biblical text whatever meaning we like, interpreting it in a wholly subjective way. On the contrary, one must reject as unauthentic every interpretation alien to the meaning expressed by the human authors in their written text. To admit the possibility of such alien meanings would be equivalent to cutting off the biblical message from its root, which is the Word of God in its historical communication; it would also mean opening the door to interpretations of a wildly subjective nature.

2. The Spiritual Sense

There are reasons, however, for not taking "alien" in so strict a sense as to exclude all possibility of higher fulfillment. The paschal event, the death and resurrection of Jesus, has established a radically new historical context, which sheds fresh light upon the ancient texts and causes them to undergo a change in meaning. In particular, certain texts which in ancient times had to be thought of as hyperbole (e.g., the oracle where God, speaking of a son of David, promised to establish his throne "forever": *2 Sam* 7:12-13; *1 Chr* 17:11-14), these texts must now be taken literally, because "Christ, having been raised from the dead, dies no more" (*Rom* 6:9). Exegetes who have a narrow, "historicist" idea about the literal sense will judge that here is an example of an interpretation alien to the original. Those who are open to the dynamic aspect of a text will recognize here a profound element of continuity as well as a move to a different level: Christ rules forever, but not on the earthly throne of David (cf also *Ps* 2:7-8; 110:1-4).

In such cases one speaks of "the spiritual sense." As a general rule, we can define the spiritual sense, as understood by Christian faith, as the meaning expressed by the biblical texts when read, under the influence of the Holy Spirit, in the context of the paschal mystery of Christ and of the new life which flows from it. This context truly exists. In it the New Testament recognizes the fulfillment of the Scriptures. It is therefore quite acceptable to re-read the Scriptures in the light of this new context, which is that of life in the Spirit.

The above definition allows us to draw some useful conclusions of a more precise nature concerning the relationship between the spiritual and literal senses:

Contrary to a current view there is not necessarily a distinction between the two senses. When a biblical text relates directly to the paschal mystery of Christ or to the new life which results from it, its literal sense is already a spiritual sense. Such is regularly the case in the New Testament. It follows that it is most often in dealing with the Old Testament that Christian exegesis speaks of the spiritual sense. But already in the Old Testament, there are many instances where texts have a religious or spiritual sense as their literal sense. Christian faith recognizes in such cases an anticipatory relationship to the new life brought by Christ.

While there is a distinction between the two senses, the spiritual sense can never be stripped of its connection with the literal sense. The latter remains the indispensable foundation.

Otherwise, one could not speak of the "fulfillment" of Scripture. Indeed, in order that there be fulfillment, a relationship of continuity and of conformity is essential. But it is also necessary that there be transition to a higher level of reality.

The spiritual sense is not to be confused with subjective interpretations stemming from the imagination or intellectual speculation. The spiritual sense results from setting the text in relation to real facts which are not foreign to it: the paschal event, in all its inexhaustible richness, which constitutes the summit of the divine intervention in the history of Israel, to the benefit of all mankind.

Spiritual interpretation, whether in community or in private, will discover the authentic spiritual sense only to the extent that it is kept within these perspectives. One then holds together three levels of reality: the biblical text, the paschal mystery and the present circumstances of life in the Spirit.

Persuaded that the mystery of Christ offers the key to interpretation of all Scripture, ancient exegesis labored to find a spiritual sense in the minutest details of the biblical text — for example, in every prescription of the ritual law — making use of rabbinic methods or inspired by Hellenistic allegorical exegesis. Whatever its pastoral usefulness might have been in the past, modern exegesis cannot ascribe true interpretative value to this kind of procedure (cf *Divino Afflante Spiritu: EB* 553).

One of the possible aspects of the spiritual sense is the typological. This is usually said to belong not to Scripture itself but to the realities expressed by Scripture: Adam as the figure of Christ (cf *Rom* 5:14), the flood as the figure of baptism (*1 Pet* 3:20-21), etc. Actually, the connection involved in typology is ordinarily based on the way in which Scripture describes the ancient reality (cf the voice of Abel: *Gen* 4:10; *Heb* 11:4; 12:24) and not simply on the reality itself. Consequently, in such a case one can speak of a meaning that is truly scriptural.

3. The Fuller Sense

The term "fuller sense" (*sensus plenior*), which is relatively recent, has given rise to discussion. The fuller sense is defined as a deeper meaning of the text, intended by God but not clearly expressed by the human author. Its existence in the biblical text comes to be known when one studies the text in the light of other biblical texts which utilize it or in its relationship with the internal development of revelation.

It is then a question either of the meaning that a subsequent biblical author attributes to an earlier biblical text, taking it up in a context which confers upon it a new literal sense, or else it is a question of the meaning that an authentic doctrinal tradition or a conciliar definition gives to a biblical text. For example, the context of *Matthew* 1:23 gives a fuller sense to the prophecy of *Isaiah* 7:14 in regard to the *almah* who will conceive, by using the translation of the Septuagint (*parthenos*): "The *virgin* will conceive." The Patristic and conciliar teaching about the Trinity expresses the fuller sense of the teaching of the New Testament regarding God the Father, the Son and the Holy Spirit. The definition of original sin by the Council of Trent provided the fuller sense of Paul's teaching in *Romans* 5:12-21 about the cons-equences of the sin of Adam for humanity. But when this kind of control — by an explicit biblical text or by an authentic doctrinal tradition — is lacking, recourse to a claimed fuller sense could lead to subjective interpretations deprived of validity.

In a word, one might think of the "fuller sense" as another way of indicating the spiritual sense of a biblical text in the case where the spiritual sense is distinct from the literal sense. It has its foundation in the fact that the Holy Spirit, principal author of the Bible, can guide human authors in the choice of expressions in such a way that the latter will express a truth the fullest depths of which the authors themselves do not perceive. This deeper truth will be more fully revealed in the course of time—on the one hand, through further divine interventions which clarify the meaning of texts and, on the other, through the insertion of texts into the canon of Scripture. In these ways there is created a new context, which brings out fresh possibilities of meaning that had lain hidden in the original context.

III. Characteristics of Catholic Interpretation

Catholic exegesis does not claim any particular scientific method as its own. It recognizes that one of the aspects of biblical texts is that they are the work of human authors, who employed both their own capacities for expression and the means which their age and social context put at their disposal. Consequently, Catholic exegesis freely makes use of the scientific methods and approaches which allow a better grasp of the meaning of texts in their linguistic, literary, socio-cultural, religious and historical contexts, while explaining them as well through studying their sources and attending to the personality of each author (cf *Divino Afflante Spiritu: EB* 557). Catholic exegesis actively contributes to the development of new methods and to the progress of research.

What characterizes Catholic exegesis is that it deliberately places itself within the living tradition of the Church, whose first concern is fidelity to the revelation attested by the Bible. Modern hermeneutics has made clear, as we have noted, the impossibility of interpreting a text without starting from a "pre-understanding" of one type or another. Catholic exegetes approach the biblical text with a pre-understanding which holds closely together modern scientific culture and the religious tradition emanating from Israel and from the early Christian community. Their interpretation stands thereby in continuity with a dynamic pattern of interpretation that is found within the Bible itself and continues in the life of the Church. This dynamic pattern corresponds to the requirement that there be a lived affinity between the interpreter and the object, an affinity which constitutes, in fact, one of the conditions that makes the entire exegetical enterprise possible.

All pre-understanding, however, brings dangers with it. As regards Catholic exegesis, the risk is that of attributing to biblical texts a meaning which they do not contain but which is the product of a later development within the tradition. The exegete must beware of such a danger.

A. Interpretation in the Biblical Tradition

The texts of the Bible are the expression of religious traditions which existed before them. The mode of their connection with these traditions is different in each case, with the creativity of the authors shown in various degrees. In the course of time, multiple traditions have flowed together little by little to form one great common tradition. The Bible is a privileged expression of this process: it has itself contributed to the process and continues to have controlling influence upon it.

The subject, "Interpretation in the Biblical Tradition," can be approached in very many ways. The expression can be taken to include the manner in which the Bible interprets fundamental human experiences or the particular events of the history of Israel, or again the manner in which the biblical texts make use of their sources, written or oral, some of which may well come from other religions or cultures — through a process of reinterpretation. But our subject is the interpretation of the

Bible; we do not want to treat here these very broad questions but simply to make some observations about the interpretation of biblical texts that occurs within the Bible itself.

1. Re-readings (Relectures)

One thing that gives the Bible an inner unity, unique of its kind, is the fact that later biblical writings often depend upon earlier ones. These more recent writings allude to older ones, create *"re-readings"* (*relectures*) which develop new aspects of meaning, sometimes quite different from the original sense. A text may also make explicit reference to older passages, whether it is to deepen their meaning or to make known their fulfillment.

Thus it is that the inheritance of the land, promised by God to Abraham for his offspring (*Gen* 15:7, 18), becomes entrance into the sanctuary of God (*Exod* 15:17), a participation in God's "rest" (*Ps* 132:7-8) reserved for those who truly have faith (*Ps* 95:8-11; *Heb* 3:7; 4:11) and, finally, entrance into the heavenly sanctuary (*Heb* 6:12; 18-20), "the eternal inheritance" (*Heb* 9:15).

The prophecy of Nathan, which promised David a "house," that is a dynastic succession, "secure forever" (*2 Sam* 7:12-16), is recalled in a number of re-phrasings (*2 Sam* 23:5; *1 Kings* 2:4; 3:6; *1 Chr* 17:11-14), arising especially out of times of distress (*Ps* 89:20-38), not without significant changes; it is continued by other prophecies (*Ps* 2:7-8; 110:1, 4; *Amos* 9:11; *Isa* 7:13-14; *Jer* 23:5-6; etc.), some of which announce the return of the kingdom of David itself (*Hos* 3:5; *Jer* 30:9; *Ezek* 34:24; 37:24-25; cf *Mark* 11:10). The promised kingdom becomes universal (*Ps* 2:8; *Dan* 2:35, 44; 7:14; cf *Matt* 28:18). It brings to fullness the vocation of human beings (*Gen* 1:28; *Ps* 8:6-9; *Wis* 9:2-3; 10:2).

The prophecy of Jeremiah concerning the 70 years of chastisement incurred by Jerusalem and Juda (*Jer* 25:11-12; 29:

10) is recalled in *2 Chronicals* 25:20-23, which affirms that this punishment has actually occurred. Nonetheless, much later, the author of *Daniel* returns to reflect upon it once more, convinced that this word of God still conceals a hidden meaning that could throw light upon the situation of his own day (*Dan* 9:24-27).

The basic affirmation of the retributive justice of God, rewarding the good and punishing the evil (*Ps* 1:1-6; 112:1-10; *Lev* 26:3-33; etc.), flies in the face of much immediate experience, which often fails to bear it out. In the face of this, Scripture allows strong voices of protestation and argument to be heard (*Ps* 44; *Job* 10:1-7; 13:3-28; 23-24), as little by little it plumbs more profoundly the full depths of the mystery (*Ps* 37; *Job* 38-42; *Isa* 53; *Wis* 3-5).

2. Relationships between the Old Testament and the New

Intertextual relationships become extremely dense in the writings of the New Testament, thoroughly imbued as it is with the Old Testament through both multiple allusion and explicit citation. The authors of the New Testament accorded to the Old Testament the value of divine revelation. They proclaimed that this revelation found its fulfillment in the life, in the teaching and above all in the death and resurrection of Jesus, source of pardon and of everlasting life. "Christ died for our sins *according to the Scriptures* and was buried; he was raised on the third day *according to the Scriptures* and appeared..." (*1 Cor* 15:3-5): such is the center and core of the apostolic preaching (*1 Cor* 15:11).

As always, the relationship between Scripture and the events which bring it to fulfillment is not one of simple material correspondence. On the contrary, there is mutual illumination and a progress that is dialectic: what becomes clear is that Scripture reveals the meaning of events and that events reveal the meaning of Scripture, that is, they require that certain aspects of the received interpretation be set aside and a new interpretation adopted.

Right from the start of his public ministry, Jesus adopted a personal and original stance different from the accepted interpretation of his age, that "of the scribes and Pharisees" *(Matt* 5:20). There is ample evidence of this: the antitheses of his Sermon on the Mount *(Matt* 5:21-48); his sovereign freedom with respect to Sabbath observance *(Mark* 2:27-28 and parallels); his way of relativizing the precepts of ritual purity *(Mark* 7:1-23 and parallels); on the other hand, the radicality of his demand in other areas *(Matt* 10:2-12 and parallels; 10:17-27 and parallels) and, above all, his attitude of welcome to "the tax-collectors and sinners" *(Mark* 2:15-17 and parallels). All this was in no sense the result of a personal whim to challenge the established order. On the contrary, it represented a most profound fidelity to the will of God expressed in Scripture (cf *Matt* 5:17; 9:13; *Mark* 7:8-13 and parallels; 10:5-9 and parallels).

Jesus' death and resurrection pushed to the very limit the interpretative development he had begun, provoking on certain points a complete break with the past, alongside unforeseen new openings. The death of the Messiah, "king of the Jews" *(Mark* 15:26 and parallels), prompted a transformation of the purely earthly interpretation of the royal psalms and messianic prophecies. The resurrection and heavenly glorification of Jesus as Son of God lent these texts a fullness of meaning previously unimaginable. The result was that some expressions which had seemed to be hyperbole had now to be taken literally. They came to be seen as divine preparations to express the glory of Christ Jesus, for Jesus is truly "Lord" *(Ps* 110:1), in the fullest sense of the word *(Acts* 2:3-6; *Phil* 2:10-11; *Heb* 1:10-12); he is Son of God *(Ps* 2:7; *Mark* 14:62; *Rom* 1:3-4), God with God *(Ps* 45:7;

Heb 1:8; *John* 1:1; 20:28); "his reign will have no end" (*Luke* 1:32-33; cf *1 Chr* 17:11-14; *Ps* 45:7; *Heb* 1:8) and he is at the same time "priest forever" (*Ps* 110:4; *Heb* 5:6-10; 7:23-24).

It is in the light of the events of Easter that the authors of the New Testament read anew the scriptures of the Old. The Holy Spirit, sent by the glorified Christ (cf *John* 15:26; 16:7), led them to discover the spiritual sense. While this meant that they came to stress more than ever the prophetic value of the Old Testament, it also had the effect of relativizing very considerably its value as a system of salvation. This second point of view, which already appears in the Gospels (cf *Matt* 11:11-13 and parallels; 12:41-42 and parallels; *John* 4:12-14; 5:37; 6:32), emerges strongly in certain Pauline letters as well as in the *Letter to the Hebrews*. Paul and the author of the *Letter to the Hebrews* show that the Torah itself, insofar as it is revelation, announces its own proper end as a legal system (cf *Gal* 2:15 — 5:1; *Rom* 3:20-21; 6:14; *Heb* 7:11-19; 10:8-9). It follows that the pagans who adhere to faith in Christ need not be obliged to observe all the precepts of biblical law, from now on reduced in its entirety simply to the status of a legal code of a particular people. But in the Old Testament as the Word of God they have to find the spiritual sustenance that will assist them to discover the full dimensions of the paschal mystery which now governs their lives (cf *Luke* 24:25-27, 44-45; *Rom* 1:1-2).

All this serves to show that within the one Christian Bible, the relationships that exist between the New and the Old Testament are quite complex. When it is a question of the use of particular texts, the authors of the New Testament naturally have recourse to the ideas and procedures for interpretation current in their time. To require them to conform to modern scientific methods would be anachronistic. Rather, it is for the exegete to acquire a knowledge of ancient techniques of exegesis, so as to be able to interpret correctly the way in which a scriptural author has used them. On the other hand, it remains true that the exegete need not put absolute value in something which simply reflects limited human understanding.

Finally, it is worth adding that within the New Testament, as already within the Old, one can see the juxtaposing of different perspectives that sit sometimes in tension with one another: for example, regarding the status of *Jesus* (*John* 8:29; 16:32 and *Mark* 15:34) or the value of the Mosaic Law (*Matt* 5:17-19 and *Rom* 6:14) or the necessity of works for justification (*James* 2:24 and *Rom* 3:28; *Eph* 2:8-9). One of the characteristics of the Bible is precisely the absence of a sense of systematization and the presence, on the contrary, of things held in dynamic tension. The Bible is a repository of many ways of interpreting the same events and reflecting upon the same problems. In itself it urges us to avoid excessive simplification and narrowness of spirit.

3. Some Conclusions

From what has just been said, one can conclude that the Bible contains numerous indications and suggestions relating to the art of interpretation. In fact, from its very inception the Bible has been itself a work of interpretation. Its texts were recognized by the communities of the Former Covenant and by those of the apostolic age as the genuine expression of the common faith. It is in accordance with the interpretative work of these communities and together with it that the texts were accepted as Sacred Scripture (thus, e.g., the *Song of Songs* was recognized as Sacred Scripture when applied to the relation between God and Israel). In the course of the Bible's formation, the writings of which it consists were in many cases reworked and reinterpreted, so as to make them respond to new situations, previously unknown.

The way in which Sacred Scripture reveals its own

interpretation of texts suggests the following observations:

Sacred Scripture has come into existence on the basis of a consensus in the believing communities recognizing in the texts the expression of revealed faith. This means that, for the living faith of the ecclesial communities, the interpretation of Scripture should itself be a source of consensus on essential matters.

Granted that the expression of faith, such as it is found in the Sacred Scripture acknowledged by all, has had to renew itself continually in order to meet new situations — which explains the "re-readings" of many of the biblical texts — the interpretation of the Bible should likewise involve an aspect of creativity; it ought also to confront new questions, so as to respond to them out of the Bible.

Granted that tensions can exist in the relationship between various texts of Sacred Scripture, interpretation must necessarily show a certain pluralism. No single interpretation can exhaust the meaning of the whole, which is a symphony of many voices. Thus the interpretation of one particular text has to avoid seeking to dominate at the expense of others.

Sacred Scripture is in dialogue with communities of believers: it has come from their traditions of faith. Its texts have been developed in relation to these traditions and have contributed, reciprocally, to the development of the traditions. It follows that interpretation of Scripture takes place in the heart of the Church: in its plurality and its unity, and within its tradition of faith.

Faith traditions formed the living context for the literary activity of the authors of Sacred Scripture. Their insertion into this context also involved a sharing in both the liturgical and external life of the communities, in their intellectual world, in their culture and in the ups and downs of their shared history. In like manner, the interpretation of Sacred Scripture requires full participation on the part of exegetes in the life and faith of the believing community of their own time.

Dialogue with Scripture in its entirety, which means dialogue with the understanding of the faith prevailing in earlier times, must be matched by a dialogue with the generation of today. Such dialogue will mean establishing a relationship of continuity. It will also involve acknowledging differences. Hence the interpretation of Scripture involves a work of sifting and setting aside; it stands in continuity with earlier exegetical traditions, many elements of which it preserves and makes its own; but in other matters it will go its own way, seeking to make further progress.

B. Interpretation in the Tradition of the Church

The Church, as the People of God, is aware that it is helped by the Holy Spirit in its understanding and interpretation of Scripture. The first disciples of Jesus knew that they did not have the capacity right away to understand the full reality of what they had received in all its aspects. As they persevered in their life as a community, they experienced an ever-deepening and progressive clarification of the revelation they had received. They recognized in this the influence and the action of "the Spirit of truth," which Christ had promised them, to guide them to the fullness of the truth (*John* 16:12-13). Likewise the Church today journeys onward, sustained by the promise of Christ: "The Paraclete, the Holy Spirit, which the Father will send in my name, will teach you all things and will make you recall all that I have said to you" (*John* 14:26).

1. Formation of the Canon

Guided by the Holy Spirit and in the light of the living Tradition which it has received, the Church has discerned the writings which should be regarded as Sacred Scripture in the sense that, "having been written under the inspiration of the Holy Spirit, they have God as their author and have been handed on as such to the Church" (*Dei Verbum*, 11) and contain "that truth which God wanted put into the Sacred Writings for the sake of our salvation" (*ibid.*).

The discernment of a "canon" of Sacred Scripture was the result of a long process. The communities of the Old Covenant (ranging from particular groups, such as those connected with prophetic circles or the priesthood, to the people as a whole) recognized in a certain number of texts the Word of God capable of arousing their faith and providing guidance for daily life; they received these texts as a patrimony to be preserved and handed on. In this way these texts ceased to be merely the expression of a particular author's inspiration; they became the common property of the whole people of God. The New Testament attests its own reverence for these sacred texts, received as a precious heritage passed on by the Jewish people. It regards these texts as "Sacred Scripture" (*Rom* 1:2), "inspired" by the Spirit of God (*2 Tim* 3:16; cf *2 Pet* 1:20-21), which "can never be annulled" (*John* 10:35).

To these texts, which form "the Old Testament" (cf *2 Cor* 3:14), the Church has closely associated other writings: first, those in which it recognized the authentic witness, coming from the apostles (cf *Luke* 1:2; *1 John* 1:1-3) and guaranteed by the Holy Spirit (cf *1 Pet* 1:12), concerning "all that Jesus began to do and teach" (*Acts* 1:1) and, secondly, the instructions given by the apostles themselves and other disciples for the building up of the community of believers. This double series of writings subsequently came to be known as "the New Testament."

Many factors played a part in this process: the conviction that Jesus — and the apostles along with him — had recognized the Old Testament as inspired Scripture and that the paschal mystery is its true fulfillment; the conviction that the writings of the New Testament were a genuine reflection of the apostolic preaching (which does not imply that they were all composed by the apostles themselves); the recognition of their conformity with the rule of faith and of their use in the Christian liturgy; finally, the experience of their affinity with the ecclesial life of the communities and of their potential for sustaining this life.

In discerning the canon of Scripture, the Church was also discerning and defining her own identity. Henceforth Scripture was to function as a mirror in which the Church could continually rediscover her identity and assess, century after century, the way in which she constantly responds to the gospel and equips herself to be an apt vehicle of its transmission (cf *Dei Verbum*, 7). This confers on the canonical writings a salvific and theological value completely different from that attaching to other ancient texts. The latter may throw much light on the origins of the faith. But they can never substitute for the authority of the writings held to be canonical and thus fundamental for the understanding of the Christian faith.

2. Patristic Exegesis

From earliest times it has been understood that the same Holy Spirit, who moved the authors of the New Testament to put in writing the message of salvation (*Dei Verbum*, 7; 18), likewise provided the Church with continual assistance for the interpretation of its inspired writings (cf Irenaeus, *Adv. Haer.*, 3.24.1; cf 3.1.1; 4.33.8; Origen, *De Princ.*, 2.7.2; Tertullian, *De Praescr.*, 22).

The Fathers of the Church, who had a particular role in the process of the formation of the canon, likewise have a foundational role in relation to the living tradition which unceasingly accompanies and guides the Church's reading and interpretation of Scripture (cf *Providentissimus: EB* 110-111; *Divino Afflante Spiritu,* 28-30: *EB* 554; *Dei Verbum,* 23; *PCB, Instr, de Evang. histor.,* 1). Within the broader current of the great Tradition, the particular contribution of patristic exegesis consists in this: to have drawn out from the totality of Scripture the basic orientations which shaped the doctrinal tradition of the Church, and to have provided a rich theological teaching for the instruction and spiritual sustenance of the faithful.

The Fathers of the Church placed a high value upon the reading of Scripture and its interpretation. This can be seen, first of all, in works directly linked to the understanding of Scripture, such as homilies and commentaries. But it is also evident in works of controversy and theology, where appeal is made to Scripture in support of the main argument.

For the Fathers the chief occasion for reading the Bible is in church, in the course of the liturgy. This is why the interpretations they provide are always of a theological and pastoral nature, touching upon relationship with God, so as to be helpful both for the community and the individual believer.

The Fathers look upon the Bible above all as the Book of God, the single work of a single author. This does not mean, however, that they reduce the human authors to nothing more than passive instruments; they are quite capable, also, of according to a particular book its own specific purpose. But their type of approach pays scant attention to the historical development of revelation. Many Fathers of the Church present the *Logos,* the Word of God, as author of the Old Testament and in this way insist that all Scripture has a christological meaning.

Setting aside certain exegetes of the School of Antioch (Theodore of Mopsuestia, in particular), the Fathers felt themselves at liberty to take a sentence out of its context in order to bring out some revealed truth which they found expressed within it. In apologetic directed against Jewish positions or in theological dispute with other theologians, they did not hesitate to rely on this kind of interpretation.

Their chief concern being to live from the Bible in communion with their brothers and sisters, the Fathers were usually content to use the text of the Bible current in their own context. What led Origen to take a systematic interest in the Hebrew Bible was a concern to conduct arguments with Jews from texts which the latter found acceptable. Thus, in his praise for the *hebraica veritas,* St. Jerome appears, in this respect, a somewhat untypical figure.

As a way of eliminating the scandal which particular passages of the Bible might provide for certain Christians, not to mention pagan adversaries of Christianity, the Fathers had recourse fairly frequently to the allegorical method. But they rarely abandoned the literalness and historicity of texts. The Fathers' recourse to allegory transcends for the most part a simple adaptation to the allegorical method in use among pagan authors.

Recourse to allegory stems also from the conviction that the Bible, as God's book, was given by God to his people, the Church. In principle, there is nothing in it which is to be set aside as out of date or completely lacking meaning. God is constantly speaking to his Christian people a message that is ever relevant for their time. In their explanations of the Bible, the Fathers mix and weave together typological and allegorical interpretations in a virtually inextricable way. But they do so always for a pastoral and pedagogical purpose, convinced that everything that has been written, has been written for our instruction (cf *1 Cor* 10:11).

Convinced that they are dealing with the book of God and therefore with something of inexhaustible meaning, the Fathers hold that any particular passage is open to any particular interpretation on an allegorical basis. But they also consider that others are free to offer something else, provided only that what is offered respects the analogy of faith.

The allegorical interpretation of Scripture so characteristic of patristic exegesis runs the risk of being something of an embarrassment to people today. But the experience of the Church expressed in this exegesis makes a contribution that is always useful (cf *Divino Afflante Spiritu,* 31-32; *Dei Verbum,* 23). The Fathers of the Church teach to read the Bible theologically, within the heart of a living Tradition, with an authentic Christian spirit.

3. The Roles of Various Members of the Church in Interpretation

The Scriptures, as given to the Church, are the communal treasure of the entire body of believers: "Sacred Tradition and Sacred Scripture form one sacred deposit of the Word of God, entrusted to the Church. Holding fast to this deposit, the entire holy people, united with its pastors, remains steadfastly faithful to the teaching of the apostles..." (*Dei Verbum,* 10; cf also 21). It is true that the familiarity with the text of Scripture has been more notable among the faithful at some periods of the Church's history than in others. But Scripture has been at the forefront of all the important moments of renewal in the life of the Church, from the Monastic movement of the early centuries to the recent era of the Second Vatican Council.

This same Council teaches that all the baptized, when they bring their faith in Christ to the celebration of the Eucharist, recognize the presence of Christ also in his word, "for it is he himself who speaks when the holy scriptures are read in the

Church" (*Sacrosanctum Concilium,* 7). To this hearing of the word, they bring that "sense of the faith" (*sensus fidei*) which characterizes the entire People (of God).... For by this sense of faith "aroused and sustained by the Spirit of truth, the People of God, guided by the sacred Magisterium which it faithfully follows, accepts not a human word but the very Word of God (cf *1 Thess* 2:13). It holds fast unerringly to the faith once delivered to the saints (cf *Jude* 3), it penetrates it more deeply with accurate insight and applies it more thoroughly to Christian life" (*Lumen Gentium,* 12).

Thus all the members of the Church have a role in the interpretation of Scripture. In the exercise of their pastoral ministry, *bishops,* as successors of the apostles, are the first witnesses and guarantors of the living tradition within which Scripture is interpreted in every age. "Enlightened by the Spirit of truth, they have the task of guarding faithfully the Word of God, of explaining it and through their preaching making it more widely known" (*Dei Verbum,* 9; cf *Lumen Gentium,* 25). As co-workers with the bishops, *priests* have as their primary duty the proclamation of the Word (*Presbyterorum Ordinis,* 4). They are gifted with a particular charism for the interpretation of Scripture, when, transmitting not their own ideas, but the Word of God, they apply the eternal truth of the Gospel to the concrete circumstances of daily life (*ibid.*). It belongs to *priests* and to *deacons,* especially when they administer the sacraments, to make clear the unity constituted by Word and Sacrament in the ministry of the Church.

As those who preside at the eucharistic community and as educators in the faith, the ministers of the Word have as their principal task, not simply to impart instruction, but also to assist the faithful to understand and discern what the Word of God is saying to them in their hearts when they hear and reflect upon the

Scriptures. Thus the *local church* as a whole, on the pattern of Israel, the People of God (*Exod* 19:5-6), becomes a community which knows that it is addressed by God (cf *John* 6:45), a community that listens eagerly to the Word with faith, love and docility (*Deut* 6:4-6). Granted that they remain ever united in faith and love with the wider body of the Church, such truly-listening communities become in their own context vigorous sources of evangelization and of dialogue, as well as agents for social change (*Evangelii nuntiandi*, 57-58; *CDF*, *Instruction Concerning Christian Freedom and Liberation*, 69-70).

The Spirit is, assuredly, also given to *individual Christians,* so that their hearts can "burn within them" (*Luke* 24:32), as they pray and prayerfully study the Scripture within the context of their own personal lives. This is why the Second Vatican Council insisted that access to Scripture be facilitated in every possible way (*Dei Verbum,* 22; 25), This kind of reading, it should be noted, is never completely private, for the believer always reads and interprets Scripture within the faith of the Church and then brings back to the community the fruit of that reading, for the enrichment of the common faith.

The entire biblical tradition and, in a particular way, the teaching of Jesus in the Gospels indicates as privileged hearers of the Word of God those whom the world considers *people of lowly status.* Jesus acknowledged that things hidden from the wise and learned have been revealed to the simple (*Matt* 11:25; *Luke* 10:21) and that the Kingdom of God belongs to those who make themselves like little children (*Mark* 10:14 and parallels).

Likewise, Jesus proclaimed: "Blessed are you poor, because the Kingdom of God is yours" (*Luke* 6:20; cf *Matt* 5:3). One of the signs of the messianic era is the proclamation of the Good News to the poor (*Luke* 4:18; 7:22; *Matt* 11:5; cf *CDF*, *Instruction Concerning Christian Freedom and Liberation,* 47-

48). Those who, in their powerlessness and lack of human resources, find themselves forced to put their trust in God alone and in his justice have a capacity for hearing and interpreting the Word of God which should be taken into account by the whole Church; it demands a response on the social level as well.

Recognizing the diversity of gifts and functions which the Spirit places at the service of the community, especially the gift of teaching (*1 Cor* 12:28-30; *Rom* 12:6-7; *Eph* 4:11-16), the Church expresses its esteem for those who display a particular ability to contribute to the building up of the Body of Christ through their expertise in interpreting Scripture *(Divino Afflante Spiritu,* 46-48: *EB* 564-565; *Dei Verbum*, 23; *PCB*, *Instruction Concerning the Historical Truth of the Gospels,* Introd.). Although their labors did not always receive in the past the encouragement that is given them today, *exegetes* who offer their learning as a service to the Church find that they are part of a rich tradition which stretches from the first centuries, with Origen and Jerome, up to more recent times, with Père Lagrange and others, and continues right up to our time. In particular, the discovery of the literal sense of Scripture, upon which there is now so much insistence, requires the combined efforts of those who have expertise in the fields of ancient languages, of history and culture, of textual criticism and the analysis of literary forms, and who know how to make good use of the methods of scientific criticism. Beyond this attention to the text in its original historical context, the Church depends on exegetes, animated by the same Spirit as inspired Scripture, to ensure that "there be as great a number of servants of the Word of God as possible capable of effectively providing the people of God with the nourishment of the Scriptures" (*Divino Afflante Spiritu,* 24; 53-55: *EB* 551, 567; *Dei Verbum*, 23; Paul VI, *Sedula Cura* [1971]). A particular cause for satisfaction in our times is the growing number of *women exegetes*; they frequently contribute new and penetrating insights to the interpretation of Scripture and rediscover features which had been forgotten.

If, as noted above, the Scriptures belong to the entire Church and are part of "the heritage of the faith," which all, pastors and faithful, "preserve, profess and put into practice in a communal effort," it nevertheless remains true that "responsibility for authentically interpreting the Word of God, as transmitted by Scripture and Tradition, has been entrusted solely to the living Magisterium of the Church, which exercises its authority in the name of Jesus Christ" (*Dei Verbum,* 10). Thus, in the last resort it is the Magisterium which has the responsibility of guaranteeing the authenticity of interpretation and, should the occasion arise, of pointing out instances where any particular interpretation is incompatible with the authentic Gospel. It discharges this function within the *koinonia* of the Body, expressing officially the faith of the Church, as a service to the Church; to this end it consults theologians, exegetes and other experts, whose legitimate liberty it recognizes and with whom it remains united by reciprocal relationship in the common goal of "preserving the people of God in the truth which sets them free" (*CDF, Instruction Concerning the Ecclesial Vocation of the Theologian,* 21).

C. The Task of the Exegete

The task of Catholic exegetes embraces many aspects. It is an ecclesial task, for it consists in the study and explanation of Holy Scripture in a way that makes all its riches available to pastors and the faithful. But it is at the same time a work of scholarship, which places the Catholic exegete in contact with non-Catholic colleagues and with many areas of scholarly research. Moreover, this task includes at the same time both research and teaching. And each of these normally leads to publication.

1. Principal Guidelines

In devoting themselves to their task, Catholic exegetes have to pay due account to the *historical character* of biblical revelation. For the two Testaments express in human words bearing the stamp of their time the historical revelation communicated by God in various ways, concerning himself and his plan of salvation. Consequently, exegetes have to make use of the historical-critical method. They cannot, however, accord to it a sole validity. All methods pertaining to the interpretation of texts are entitled to make their contribution to the exegesis of the Bible.

In their work of interpretation, Catholic exegetes must never forget that what they are interpreting is the *Word of God*. Their common task is not finished when they have simply determined sources, defined forms or explained literary procedures. They arrive at the true goal of their work only when they have explained the meaning of the biblical text as God's word for today. To this end, they must take into consideration the various hermeneutical perspectives which help toward grasping the contemporary meaning of the biblical message and which make it responsive to the needs of those who read Scripture today.

Exegetes should also explain the christological, canonical and ecclesial meanings of the biblical texts.

The *christological* significance of biblical texts is not always evident; it must be made clear whenever possible. Although Christ established the New Covenant in his blood, the books of the First Covenant have not lost their value. Assumed into the proclamation of the Gospel, they acquire and display their full meaning in the "mystery of Christ" (*Eph* 3:4); they shed light upon multiple aspects of this mystery, while in turn being illuminated by it themselves. These writings, in fact, served to prepare the people of God for his coming (cf *Dei Verbum*, 14-16).

106

Although each book of the Bible was written with its own particular end in view and has its own specific meaning, it takes on a deeper meaning when it becomes part of the *canon* as a whole. The exegetical task includes therefore bringing out the truth of Augustine's dictum:

"*Novum Testamentum in Vetere latet,*
et in Novo Vetus patet"
["The New Testament lies hidden in the Old,
and the Old becomes clear in the New"]
(cf *Quaest. in Hept.*, 2, 73: *CSEL* 28, III, 3, p. 141).

Exegetes have also to explain the relationship that exists between the Bible and the *Church*. The Bible came into existence within believing communities. In it the faith of Israel found expression, later that of the early Christian communities. United to the living Tradition which preceded it, which accompanies it and is nourished by it (cf *Dei Verbum,* 21), the Bible is the privileged means which God uses yet again in our own day to shape the budding up and the growth of the Church as the People of God. This ecclesial dimension necessarily involves an openness to ecumenism.

Moreover, since the Bible tells of God's offer of salvation to all people, the exegetical task necessarily includes a universal dimension. This means taking account of other religions and of the hopes and fears of the world of today.

2. Research

The exegetical task is far too large to be successfully pursued by individual scholars working alone. It calls for a division of labor, especially in *research*, which demands specialists in different fields. Interdisciplinary collaboration will help overcome any limitations that specialization may tend to produce.

It is very important for the good of the entire Church, as well as for its influence in the modern world, that a sufficient number of well-prepared persons be committed to research in the various fields of exegetical study. In their concern for the more immediate needs of the ministry, bishops and religious superiors are often tempted not to take sufficiently seriously the responsibility incumbent upon them to make provision for this fundamental need. But a lack in this area exposes the Church to serious harm, for pastors and the faithful then run the risk of being at the mercy of an exegetical scholarship which is alien to the Church and lacks relationship to the life of faith. In stating that "the *study* of Sacred Scripture" should be "as it were the soul of theology" (*Dei Verbum,* 24), the Second Vatican Council has indicated the crucial importance of exegetical research. By the same token, the Council has also implicitly reminded Catholic exegetes that their research has an essential relationship to theology, their awareness of which must also be evident.

3. Teaching

The declaration of the Council made equally clear the fundamental role which belongs to the *teaching* of exegesis in the faculties of theology, the seminaries and the religious houses of studies. It is obvious that the level of these studies will not be the same in all cases. It is desirable that the teaching of exegesis be carried out by both men and women. More technical in university faculties, this teaching will have a more directly pastoral orientation in seminaries. But it can never be without an intellectual dimension that is truly serious. To proceed otherwise would be to show disrespect toward the Word of God.

Professors of exegesis should communicate to their students a profound appreciation of Sacred Scripture, showing how it deserves the kind of attentive and objective study which will allow a better appreciation of its literary, historical, social and theological value. They cannot rest content simply with the conveying of a series of facts to be passively absorbed but should give a genuine introduction to exegetical method, explaining the principal steps, so that students will be in a position to exercise their own personal judgment.

Given the limited time at a teacher's disposal, it is appropriate to make use of two alternative modes of teaching: on the one hand, a synthetic exposition to introduce the student to the study of whole books of the Bible, omitting no important area of the Old or New Testament; on the other hand, in-depth analyses of certain, well-chosen texts, which will provide at the same time an introduction to the practice of exegesis. In either case, care must be taken to avoid a one-sided approach that would restrict itself, on the one hand, to a spiritual commentary empty of historical-critical grounding or, on the other, to a historical-critical commentary lacking doctrinal or spiritual content (cf *Divino Afflante Spiritu: EB* 551-552; *PCB, De Sacra Scriptura recte docenda: EB* 598). Teaching should at one and the same time show forth the historical roots of the biblical writings, the way in which they constitute the personal word of the heavenly Father addressing his children with love (cf *Dei Verbum,* 21) and their indispensable role in the pastoral ministry (cf *2 Tim* 3:16).

4. Publications

As the fruit of research and a complement to teaching, publications play a highly important role in the advancement and spread of exegetical work. Beyond printed texts, publication today embraces other more powerful and more rapid means of communication (radio, television, other electronic media); it is very advantageous to know how to make use of these things.

For those engaged in research, publication at a high

academic level is the principal means of dialogue, discussion and cooperation. Through it, Catholic exegesis can interact with other centers of exegetical research as well as with the scholarly world in general.

There is another form of publication, more short-term in nature, which renders a very great service by its ability to adapt itself to a variety of readers, from the well-educated to children of catechism age, reaching biblical groups, apostolic movements and religious congregations. Exegetes who have a gift for popularization provide an extremely useful and fruitful work, one that is indispensable if the fruit of exegetical studies is to be dispersed as widely as need demands. In this area, the need to make the biblical message something real for today is ever more obvious. This requires that exegetes take into consideration the reasonable demands of educated and cultured persons of our time, clearly distinguishing for their benefit what in the Bible is to be regarded as secondary detail conditioned by a particular age, what must be interpreted as the language of myth and what is to be regarded as the true historical and inspired meaning. The biblical writings were not composed in modern language nor in the style of the 20th century. The forms of expression and literary genres employed in the Hebrew, Aramaic or Greek text must be made meaningful to men and women of today, who otherwise would be tempted to lose all interest in the Bible or else to interpret it in a simplistic way that is literalist or simply fanciful.

In all this variety of tasks, the Catholic exegete has no other purpose than the service of the Word of God. The aim of the exegete is not to substitute for the biblical texts the results of his or her work, whether that involve the reconstruction of ancient sources used by the inspired authors or up-to-date presentation of the latest conclusions of exegetical science. On the contrary, the aim of the exegete is to shed more and more light on the biblical texts themselves, helping them to be better appreciated for what they are in themselves and understood with ever more historical accuracy and spiritual depth.

D. Relationships with Other Theological Disciplines

Being itself a theological discipline, *"fides quaerens intellectum,"* exegesis has close and complex relationships with other fields of theological learning. On the one hand, systematic theology has an influence upon the presuppositions with which exegetes approach biblical texts. On the other hand, exegesis provides the other theological disciplines with data fundamental for their operation. There is, accordingly, a relationship of dialogue between exegesis and the other branches of theology, granted always a mutual respect for that which is specific to each.

1. Theology and Presuppositions Regarding Biblical Texts

Exegetes necessarily bring certain presuppositions (Fr. *précompréhension*) to biblical writings. In the case of the Catholic exegete, it is a question of presuppositions based on the certainties of faith: the Bible is a text inspired by God, entrusted to the Church for the nurturing of faith and guidance of the Christian life. These certainties of faith do not come to an exegete in an unrefined, raw state, but only as developed in the ecclesial community through the process of theological reflection. The reflection undertaken by systematic theologians upon the inspiration of Scripture and the function it serves in the life of the Church provides in this way direction for exegetical research.

But correspondingly, the work of exegetes on the inspired texts provides them with an experience which systematic theologians should take into account as they seek to explain more clearly the theology of scriptural inspiration and the interpretation of the Bible within the Church. Exegesis creates, in particular, a more lively and precise awareness of the historical character of biblical inspiration. It shows that the process of inspiration is historical, not only because it took place over the course of the history of Israel and of the early Church, but also because it came about through the agency of human beings, all of them conditioned by their time and all, under the guidance of the Spirit, playing an active role in the life of the people of God.

Moreover, theology's affirmation of the strict relationship between inspired Scripture and Tradition has been both confirmed and made more precise through the advance of exegetical study, which has led exegetes to pay increasing attention to the influence upon texts of the life-setting (*"Sitz im Leben"*) out of which they were formed.

2. Exegesis and Systematic Theology

Without being the sole *locus theologicus,* Sacred Scripture provides the privileged foundation of theological studies. In order to interpret Scripture with scholarly accuracy and precision, theologians need the work of exegetes. From their side, exegetes must orientate their research in such fashion that "the study of Sacred Scripture" can be in reality "as it were the soul of theology" (*Dei Verbum,* 24). To achieve this, they ought pay particular attention to the religious content of the biblical writings.

Exegetes can help systematic theologians avoid two extremes: on the one hand, a dualism, which would completely separate a doctrinal truth from its linguistic expression, as though the latter were of no importance; on the other hand, a fundamentalism, which, confusing the human and the divine, would consider even the contingent features of human discourse to be revealed truth.

To avoid these two extremes, it is necessary to make distinctions without at the same time making separations — thus to accept a continuing tension. The Word of God finds expression in the work of human authors. The thought and the words belong at one and the same time both to God and to human beings, in such a way that the whole Bible comes at once from God and from the inspired human author. This does not mean, however, that God has given the historical conditioning of the message a value which is absolute. It is open both to interpretation and to being brought up to date — which means being detached, to some extent, from its historical conditioning in the past and being transplanted into the historical conditioning of the present. The exegete performs the groundwork for this operation, which the systematic theologian continues by taking into account the other *loci theologici* which contribute to the development of dogma.

3. Exegesis and Moral Theology

Similar observations can be made regarding the relationship between exegesis and moral theology. The Bible closely links many instructions about proper conduct — commandments, prohibitions, legal prescriptions, prophetic exhortations and accusations, counsels of wisdom, and so forth — to the stories concerning the history of salvation. One of the tasks of exegesis consists in preparing the way for the work of moralists by assessing the significance of this wealth of material.

This task is not simple, for often the biblical texts are not concerned to distinguish universal moral principles from particular prescriptions of ritual purity and legal ordinances. All is mixed together. On the other hand, the Bible reflects a

113

considerable moral development, which finds its completion in the New Testament. It is not sufficient therefore that the Old Testament should indicate a certain moral position (e.g., the practice of slavery or of divorce, or that of extermination in the case of war) for this position to continue to have validity. One has to undertake a process of discernment. This will review the issue in the light of the progress in moral understanding and sensitivity that has occurred over the years. The writings of the Old Testament contain certain "imperfect and provisional" elements (*Dei Verbum,* 15), which the divine pedagogy could not eliminate right away. The New Testament itself is not easy to interpret in the area of morality, for it often makes use of imagery, frequently in a way that is paradoxical or even provocative; moreover, in the New Testament area the relationship between Christians and the Jewish Law is the subject of sharp controversy.

Moral theologians therefore have a right to put to exegetes many questions which will stimulate exegetical research. In many cases the response may be that no biblical text explicitly addresses the problem proposed. But even when such is the case, the witness of the Bible, taken within the framework of the forceful dynamic that governs it as a whole, will certainly indicate a fruitful direction to follow. On the most important points the moral principles of the Decalogue remain basic. The Old Testament already contains the principles and the values which require conduct in full conformity with the dignity of the human person, created "in the image of God" (*Gen* 1:27). Through the revelation of God's love that comes in Christ, the New Testament sheds the fullest light upon these principles and values.

4. Differing Points of View and Necessary Interaction

In its 1988 document on the *Interpretation of Theological Truths*, the International Theological Commission recalled that a conflict has broken out in recent times between exegesis and dogmatic theology; it then notes the positive contribution modern exegesis has made to systematic theology (*The Interpretation of Theological Truths*, 1988, C.I, 2). To be more precise, it should be said that the conflict was provoked by liberal exegesis. There was no conflict in a generalized sense between Catholic exegesis and dogmatic theology but only some instances of strong tension. It remains true, however, that tension can degenerate into conflict when, from one side or the other, differing points of view, quite legitimate in themselves, become hardened to such an extent that they become in fact irreconcilable opposites.

The points of view of both disciplines are in fact different and rightly so. The primary task of the exegete is to determine as accurately as possible the meaning of biblical texts in their own proper context, that is, first of all, in their particular literary and historical context and then in the context of the wider canon of Scripture. In the course of carrying out this task, the exegete expounds the theological meaning of texts when such a meaning is present. This paves the way for a relationship of continuity between exegesis and further theological reflection. But the point of view is not the same, for the work of the exegete is fundamentally historical and descriptive and restricts itself to the interpretation of the Bible.

Theologians as such have a role that is more speculative and more systematic in nature. For this reason, they are really interested only in certain texts and aspects of the Bible and deal, besides, with much other data which is not biblical — patristic writings, conciliar definitions, other documents of the magisterium, the liturgy — as well as systems of philosophy and the cultural, social and political situation of the contemporary world. Their task is not simply to interpret the Bible; their aim is to present an understanding of the Christian faith that bears the mark of a full reflection upon all its aspects and especially that of its crucial relationship to human existence.

Because of its speculative and systematic orientation, theology has often yielded to the temptation to consider the Bible as a store of *dicta probantia* serving to confirm doctrinal theses. In recent times, theologians have become more keenly conscious of the importance of the literary and historical context for the correct interpretation of ancient texts and they are much more ready to work in collaboration with exegetes.

Inasmuch as it is the Word of God set in writing, the Bible has a richness of meaning that no one systematic theology can ever completely capture or confine. One of the principal functions of the Bible is to mount serious challenges to theological systems and to draw attention constantly to the existence of important aspects of divine revelation and human reality which have at times been forgotten or neglected in efforts at systematic reflection. The renewal that has taken place in exegetical methodology can make its own contribution to awareness in these areas.

In a corresponding way, exegesis should allow itself to be informed by theological research. This will prompt it to put important questions to texts and so discover their full meaning and richness. The critical study of the Bible cannot isolate itself from theological research, nor from spiritual experience and the discernment of the Church. Exegesis produces its best results when it is carried out in the context of the living faith of the Christian community, which is directed toward the salvation of the entire world.

IV. Interpretation of the Bible in the Life of the Church

Exegetes may have a distinctive role in the interpretation of the Bible but they do not exercise a monopoly. This activity within the Church has aspects which go beyond the academic analysis of texts. The Church, indeed, does not regard the Bible simply as a collection of historical documents dealing with its own origins; it receives the Bible as Word of God, addressed both to itself and to the entire world at the present time. This conviction, stemming from the faith, leads in turn to the work of actualizing and inculturating the Biblical message, as well as to various uses of the inspired text in liturgy, in "Lectio divina," in pastoral ministry and in the ecumenical movement.

A. Actualization

Already within the Bible itself — as we noted in the previous chapter — one can point to instances of actualization: very early texts have been re-read in the light of new circumstances and applied to the contemporary situation of the People of God. The same basic conviction necessarily stimulates believing communities of today to continue the process of actualization.

1. Principles

Actualization rests on the following basic principles:

Actualization is possible because the richness of meaning contained in the biblical text gives it a value for all time and all cultures (cf *Isa* 40:8; 66:18-21; *Matt* 28:19-20). The biblical message can at the same time both relativize and enrich the value systems and norms of behavior of each generation.

Actualization is necessary because, although their message

is of lasting value, the biblical texts have been composed with respect to circumstances of the past and in language conditioned by a variety of times and seasons. To reveal their significance for men and women of today, it is necessary to apply their message to contemporary circumstances and to express it in language adapted to the present time. This presupposes a hermeneutical endeavor, the aim of which is to go beyond the historical conditioning so as to determine the essential points of the message.

The work of actualization should always be conscious of the complex relationships that exist in the Christian Bible between the two Testaments, since the New Testament presents itself, at one and the same time, as both the fulfillment and the surpassing of the Old. Actualization takes place in line with the dynamic unity thus established.

It is the living tradition of the community of faith that stimulates the task of actualization. This community places itself in explicit continuity with the communities which gave rise to Scripture and which preserved and handed it on. In the process of actualization, tradition plays a double role: on the one hand, it provides protection against deviant interpretations; on the other hand, it ensures the transmission of the original dynamism.

Actualization, therefore, cannot mean manipulation of the text. It is not a matter of projecting novel opinions or ideologies upon the biblical writings, but of sincerely seeking to discover what the text has to say at the present time. The text of the Bible has authority over the Christian Church at all times, and, although centuries have passed since the time of its composition, the text retains its role of privileged guide not open to manipulation. The Magisterium of the Church "is not above the Word of God, but serves it, teaching only what has been handed on; by divine commission, with the help of the Holy Spirit, the Church listens to the text with love, watches over it in holiness and explains it faithfully" (*Dei Verbum*, 10).

2. Methods

Based on these principles, various methods of actualization are available.

Actualization, already practiced within the Bible itself, was continued in the Jewish tradition through procedures found in the Targums and Midrashim: searching for parallel passages (*gezerah shawah*), modification in the reading of the text (*'al tiqrey*), appropriation of a second meaning (*tartey mishma'*), etc.

In their turn, the Fathers of the Church made use of typology and allegory in order to actualize the biblical text in a manner appropriate to the situation of Christians of their time.

Modern attempts at actualization should keep in mind both changes in ways of thinking and the progress made in interpretative method.

Actualization presupposes a correct exegesis of the text, part of which is the determining of its *literal sense*. Persons engaged in the work of actualization who do not themselves have training in exegetical procedures should have recourse to good introductions to Scripture; this will ensure that their interpretation proceeds in the right direction.

The most sure and promising method for arriving at a successful actualization, is the interpretation of Scripture by Scripture, especially in the case of the texts of the Old Testament which have been re-read in the Old Testament itself (e.g., the manna of *Exodus* 16 in *Wis* 16:20-29) and/or in the New Testament (*John* 6). The actualization of a biblical text in Christian life will proceed correctly only in relation to the mystery of Christ and of the Church. It would be inappropriate, for example, to propose to Christians as models of a struggle for liberation, episodes drawn solely from the Old Testament (*Exodus*; *1-2 Maccabees*).

Based upon various forms of the philosophy of hermeneutics, the task of interpretation involves, accordingly, three steps: 1. to hear the Word from within one's own concrete situation; 2. to identify the aspects of the present situation highlighted or put in question by the biblical text; 3. to draw from the fullness of meaning contained in the biblical text those elements capable of advancing the present situation in a way that is productive and consonant with the saving will of God in Christ.

By virtue of actualization, the Bible can shed light upon many current issues: for example, the question of various forms of ministry, the sense of the Church as communion, the preferential option for the poor, liberation theology, the situation of women. Actualization can also attend to values of which the modern world is more and more conscious, such as the rights of the human person, the protection of human life, the preservation of nature, the longing for world peace.

3. Limits

So as to remain in agreement with the saving truth expressed in the Bible, the process of actualization should keep within certain limits and be careful not to take wrong directions.

While every reading of the Bible is necessarily selective, care should be taken to avoid *tendentious interpretations*, that is, readings which, instead of being docile to the text, make use of it only for their own narrow purposes (as is the case in the actualization practiced by certain sects, for example, Jehovah's Witnesses).

Actualization loses all validity if it is grounded in *theoretical principles* which are at variance with the fundamental orientations of the Biblical text, as, for example, a rationalism which is opposed to faith or an atheistic materialism.

Clearly to be rejected also is every attempt at actualization set in a direction contrary to *evangelical justice and charity*, such as, for example, the use of the Bible to justify racial segregation, anti-Semitism or sexism whether on the part of men or of women. Particular attention is necessary, according to the spirit of the Second Vatican Council (*Nostra Aetate,* 4), to avoid absolutely any actualization of certain texts of the New Testament which could provoke or reinforce unfavorable attitudes to the Jewish people. The tragic events of the past must, on the contrary, impel all to keep unceasingly in mind that, according to the New Testament, the Jews remain "beloved" of God, "since the gifts and calling of God are irrevocable" (*Rom* 11:28-29).

False paths will be avoided if actualization of the biblical message begins with a correct interpretation of the text and continues within the stream of the living Tradition, under the guidance of the Church's Magisterium.

In any case, the risk of error does not constitute a valid objection against performing what is a necessary task: that of bringing the message of the Bible to the ears and hearts of people of our own time.

B. Inculturation

While actualization allows the Bible to remain fruitful at different periods, inculturation in a corresponding way looks to the diversity of place: it ensures that the biblical message take root in a great variety of terrain. This diversity is, to be sure, never total. Every authentic culture is, in fact, in its own way the bearer of universal values established by God.

The theological foundation of inculturation is the conviction of faith that the Word of God transcends the cultures in which it has found expression and has the capability of being spread in other cultures, in such a way as to be able to reach all human beings in the cultural context in which they live. This conviction springs from the Bible itself, which, right from the book of *Genesis*, adopts a universalist stance (*Gen* 1:27-28), maintains it subsequently in the blessing promised to all peoples through Abraham and his offspring (*Gen* 12:3; 18:18) and confirms it definitively in extending to "all nations" the proclamation of the Christian gospel (*Matt* 28:18-20; *Rom* 4:16-17; *Eph* 3:6).

The first stage of inculturation consists in *translating* the inspired Scripture into another language. This step was taken already in the Old Testament period, when the Hebrew text of the Bible was translated orally into Aramaic (*Neh* 8:8, 12) and later in written form into Greek. A translation, of course, is always more than a simple transcription of the original text. The passage from one language to another necessarily involves a change of cultural context: concepts are not identical and symbols have a different meaning, for they come up against other traditions of thought and other ways of life.

Written in Greek, the New Testament is characterized in its entirety by a dynamic of inculturation. In its transposition of the Palestinian message of Jesus into Judeo-Hellenistic culture it displays its intention to transcend the limits of a single cultural world.

While it may constitute the basic step, the translation of biblical texts cannot, however, ensure by itself a thorough inculturation. Translation has to be followed by *interpretation,* which should set the biblical message in more explicit relationship with the ways of feeling, thinking, living and self-expression which are proper to the local culture. From interpretation, one passes then to other stages of inculturation, which lead to the formation of a local Christian culture, extending to all aspects of life (prayer, work, social life, customs, legislation, arts and sciences, philosophical and theological reflection). The Word of God is, in effect, a seed, which extracts from the earth in which it is planted the elements which are useful for its growth and fruitfulness (cf *Ad Gentes,* 22). As a consequence, Christians must try to discern "what riches God, in his generosity, has bestowed on the nations; at the same time they should try to shed the light of the Gospel on these treasures, to set them free and bring them under the dominion of God the Savior" (*Ad Gentes*, 11).

This is not, as is clear, a one-way process; it involves "mutual enrichment." On the one hand, the treasures contained in diverse cultures allow the Word of God to produce new fruits and, on the other hand, the light of the Word allows for a certain selectivity with respect to what cultures have to offer: harmful elements can be left aside and the development of valuable ones encouraged. Total fidelity to the person of Christ, to the dynamic of his paschal mystery and to his love for the Church, make it possible to avoid two false solutions: a superficial "adaptation" of the message, on the one hand, and a syncretistic confusion, on the other (*Ad Gentes*, 22).

Inculturation of the Bible has been carried out from the first centuries, both in the Christian East and in the Christian West, and it has proved very fruitful. However, one can never consider it a task achieved. It must be taken up again and again, in relationship to the way in which cultures continue to evolve. In countries of more recent evangelization, the problem arises in somewhat different terms. Missionaries, in fact, cannot help bring the Word of God in the form in which it has been inculturated in their own country of origin. New local churches have to make every effort to convert this foreign form of biblical inculturation into another form more closely corresponding to the culture of their own land.

C. Use of the Bible

1. In the Liturgy

From the earliest days of the Church, the reading of Scripture has been an integral part of the Christian liturgy, an inheritance to some extent from the liturgy of the Synagogue. Today, too, it is above all through the liturgy that Christians come into contact with Scripture, particularly during the Sunday celebration of the Eucharist.

In principle, the liturgy, and especially the sacramental liturgy, the high-point of which is the Eucharistic celebration, brings about the most perfect actualization of the biblical texts, for the liturgy places the proclamation in the midst of the community of believers, gathered around Christ so as to draw near to God. Christ is then "present in his word, because it is he himself who speaks when Sacred Scripture is read in the Church" (*Sacrosanctum Concilium,* 7). Written text thus becomes living word.

The liturgical reform initiated by the Second Vatican Council sought to provide Catholics with rich sustenance from the Bible. The triple cycle of Sunday readings gives a privileged place to the Gospels, in such a way as to shed light on the mystery of Christ as principle of our salvation. By regularly associating a text of the Old Testament with the text of the

Gospel, the cycle often suggests a scriptural interpretation moving in the direction of typology. But, of course, such is not the only kind of interpretation possible.

The homily, which seeks to actualize more explicitly the Word of God, is an integral part of the liturgy. We will speak of it later, when we treat of the pastoral ministry.

The lectionary, issued at the direction of the Council (*Sacrosanctum Concilium,* 35), is meant to allow for a reading of Sacred Scripture that is "more abundant, more varied and more suitable." In its present state, it only partially fulfills this goal. Nevertheless, even as it stands, it has had positive ecumenical results. In certain countries it also has served to indicate the lack of familiarity with Scripture on the part of many Catholics.

The liturgy of the Word is a crucial element in the celebration of each of the sacraments of the Church; it does not consist simply in a series of readings one after the other; it ought to involve as well periods of silence and of prayer. This liturgy, in particular the Liturgy of the Hours, makes selections from the book of *Psalms* to help the Christian community pray. Hymns and prayers are all filled with the language of the Bible and the symbolism it contains. How necessary it is, therefore, that participation in the liturgy be prepared for and accompanied by the practice of reading Scripture.

If in the readings "God addresses the word to His people" (*Roman Missal,* 33), the liturgy of the Word requires that great care be taken both in the proclamation of the readings and in their interpretation. It is therefore desirable that the formation of those who are to preside at the assembly and of those who serve with them take full account of what is required for a liturgy of the Word of God that is fully renewed. Thus, through a combined effort, the Church will carry on the mission entrusted to it, "to take the bread of life from the table both of the Word of God and of the Body of Christ and offer it to the faithful" (*Dei Verbum*, 21).

2. Lectio Divina

Lectio Divina is a reading, on an individual or communal level, of a more or less lengthy passage of Scripture, received as the Word of God and leading, at the prompting of the Spirit, to meditation, prayer and contemplation.

Concern for regular, even daily reading of Scripture reflects early Church custom. As a group practice, it is attested in the 3rd century, at the time of Origen; he used to give homilies based on a text of Scripture read continuously throughout a week. At that time there were daily gatherings devoted to the reading and explanation of Scripture. But the practice did not always meet with great success among Christians (Origen, *Hom. Gen.*, X.1) and was eventually abandoned.

Lectio Divina, especially on the part of the individual, is attested in the monastic life in its golden age. In modern times, an Instruction of the Biblical Commission, approved by Pope Pius XII, recommended this *lectio* to all clerics, secular and religious (*De Scriptura Sacra*, 1950: *EB* 592). Insistence on *Lectio Divina* in both its forms, individual and communal, has therefore become a reality once more. The end in view is to create and nourish "an efficacious and constant love" of Sacred Scripture, source of the interior life and of apostolic fruitfulness (*EB*, 591 and 567), also to promote a better understanding of the liturgy and to assure the Bible a more important place in theological studies and in prayer.

The Conciliar Constitution *Dei Verbum* (n. 25) is equally insistent on an assiduous reading of Scripture for priests and religious. Moreover — and this is something new — it also invites "all the faithful of Christ" to acquire "through frequent reading of the divine Scripture 'the surpassing knowledge of Christ Jesus'" (*Phil* 3:8). Different methods are proposed. Alongside private reading, there is the suggestion of reading in a group. The Conciliar text stresses that prayer should accompany the reading of Scripture, for prayer is the response to the Word of God encountered in Scripture under the inspiration of the Spirit. Many initiatives for communal reading have been launched among Christians and one can only encourage this desire to derive from Scripture a better knowledge of God and of his plan of salvation in Jesus Christ.

3. In Pastoral Ministry

The frequent recourse to the Bible in pastoral ministry, as recommended by *Dei Verbum* (n. 24), takes on various forms depending on the kind of interpretation that is useful to pastors and helpful for the understanding of the faithful. Three principal situations can be distinguished: catechesis, preaching and the biblical apostolate. Many factors are involved, relating to the general level of Christian life.

The explanation of the Word of God in *catechesis (Sacros. Conc.,* 35; *Gen. Catech. Direct.,* 1971, 16) has Sacred Scripture as first source. Explained in the context of the Tradition, Scripture provides the starting point, foundation and norm of catechetical teaching. One of the goals of catechesis should be to initiate a person in a correct understanding and fruitful reading of the Bible. This will bring about the discovery of the divine truth it contains and evoke as generous a response as is possible to the message God addresses through his word to the whole human race.

Catechesis should proceed from the historical context of divine revelation so as to present persons and events of the Old and New Testaments in the light of God's overall plan.

To move from the biblical text to its salvific meaning for the present time various hermeneutic procedures are employed. These will give rise to different kinds of commentary. The effectiveness of the catechesis depends on the value of the hermeneutic employed. There is the danger of resting content with a superficial commentary, one which remains simply a chronological presentation of the sequence of persons and events in the Bible.

Clearly, catechesis can avail itself of only a small part of the full range of biblical texts. Generally speaking, it will make particular use of stories, both those of the New Testament and those of the Old. It will single out the Decalogue. It should also see that it makes use of the prophetic oracles, the wisdom teaching and the great discourses in the Gospels, such as the Sermon on the Mount.

The presentation of the Gospels should be done in such a way as to elicit an encounter with Christ, who provides the key to the whole biblical revelation and communicates the call of God that summons each one to respond. The word of the prophets and that of the "ministers of the Word" (*Luke* 1:2) ought to appear as something addressed to Christians now.

Analogous remarks apply to the ministry of *preaching,* which should draw from the ancient texts spiritual sustenance adapted to the present needs of the Christian community.

Today, this ministry is exercised especially at the close of the first part of the Eucharistic celebration, through the *homily* which follows the proclamation of the Word of God.

The explanation of the biblical texts given in the course of the homily cannot enter into great detail. It is, accordingly, fitting to explain the central contribution of texts, that which is most enlightening for faith and most stimulating for the progress of the Christian life, both on the community and individual level. Presenting this central contribution means striving to achieve its actualization and inculturation, in accordance with what has been said above. Good hermeneutical principles are necessary to attain this end. Want of preparation in this area leads to the temptation to avoid plumbing the depths of the biblical readings and to being content simply to moralize or to speak of contemporary issues in a way that fails to shed upon them the light of God's Word.

In some countries exegetes have helped produce publications designed to assist pastors in their responsibility to interpret correctly the biblical texts of the liturgy and make them properly meaningful for today. It is desirable that such efforts be repeated on a wider scale.

Preachers should certainly avoid insisting in a one-sided way on the obligations incumbent upon believers. The biblical message must preserve its principal characteristic of being the good news of salvation freely offered by God. Preaching will perform a task more useful and more conformed to the Bible if it helps the faithful above all to "know the gift of God" (*John* 4:10) as it has been revealed in Scripture; they will then understand in a positive light the obligations that flow from it.

The *biblical apostolate* has as its objective to make known the Bible as the Word of God and source of life. First of all, it promotes the translation of the Bible into every kind of language and seeks to spread these translations as widely as possible. It creates and supports numerous initiatives: the formation of groups devoted to the study of the Bible, conferences on the Bible, biblical weeks, the publication of journals and books, etc.

An important contribution is made by church associations

and movements which place a high premium upon the reading of the Bible within the perspective of faith and Christian action. Many "basic Christian communities" focus their gatherings upon the Bible and set themselves a threefold objective: to know the Bible, to create community and to serve the people. Here also exegetes can render useful assistance in avoiding actualizations of the biblical message that are not well grounded in the text. But there is reason to rejoice in seeing the Bible in the hands of people of lowly condition and of the poor; they can bring to its interpretation and to its actualization a light more penetrating, from the spiritual and existential point of view, than that which comes from a learning that relies upon its own resources alone (cf *Matt* 11:25).

The ever increasing importance of the instruments of mass communication ("mass-media") — the press, radio, television — requires that proclamation of the Word of God and knowledge of the Bible be propagated by these means. Their very distinctive features and, on the other hand, their capacity to influence a vast public require a particular training in their use. This will help to avoid paltry improvisations, along with striking effects that are actually in poor taste.

Whatever be the context — catechetics, preaching or the biblical apostolate — the text of the Bible should always be presented with the respect it deserves.

4. In Ecumenism

If the ecumenical movement as a distinct and organized phenomenon is relatively recent, the idea of the unity of God's people, which this movement seeks to restore, is profoundly based in Scripture. Such an objective was the constant concern of the Lord (*John* 10:16; 17:11, 20-23). It looks to the union of

Christians in faith, hope and love (*Eph* 4:2-5), in mutual respect (*Phil* 2:1-5) and solidarity (*1 Cor* 12:14-27; *Rom* 12:4-5), but also and above all an organic union in Christ, after the manner of vine and branches (*John* 15:4-5), head and members (*Eph* 1:22-23; 4:12-16). This union should be perfect, in the likeness of the union of the Father and the Son (*John* 17:11, 22). Scripture provides its theological foundation (*Eph* 4:4-6; *Gal* 3:27-28), the first apostolic community its concrete, living model (*Acts* 2:44; 4:32).

Most of the issues which ecumenical dialogue has to confront are related in some way to the interpretation of biblical texts. Some of the issues are theological: eschatology, the structure of the Church, primacy and collegiality, marriage and divorce, the admission of women to the ministerial priesthood, and so forth. Others are of a canonical and juridical nature: they concern the administration of the universal Church and of local Churches. There are others, finally, that are strictly biblical: the list of the canonical books, certain hermeneutical questions, etc.

Although it cannot claim to resolve all these issues by itself, biblical exegesis is called upon to make an important contribution in the ecumenical area. A remarkable degree of progress has already been achieved. Through the adoption of the same methods and analogous hermeneutical points of view, exegetes of various Christian confessions have arrived at a remarkable level of agreement in the interpretation of Scripture, as is shown by the text and notes of a number of ecumenical translations of the Bible, as well as by other publications.

Indeed, it is clear that on some points differences in the interpretation of Scripture are often stimulating and can be shown to be complementary and enriching. Such is the case when these differences express values belonging to the particular tradition of various Christian communities and so convey a

131

sense of the manifold aspects of the Mystery of Christ.

Since the Bible is the common basis of the rule of faith, the ecumenical imperative urgently summons all Christians to a rereading of the inspired text, in docility to the Holy Spirit, in charity, sincerity and humility; it calls upon all to meditate on these texts and to live them in such a way as to achieve conversion of heart and sanctity of life. These two qualities, when united with prayer for the unity of Christians, constitute the soul of the entire ecumenical movement (cf *Unitatis Redintegratio*, 8). To achieve this goal, it is necessary to make the acquiring of a Bible something within the reach of as many Christians as possible, to encourage ecumenical translations — since having a common text greatly assists reading and understanding together — and also ecumenical prayer groups, in order to contribute, by an authentic and living witness, to the achievement of unity within diversity (cf *Rom* 12:4-5).

Conclusion

From what has been said in the course of this long account — admittedly far too brief on a number of points — the first conclusion that emerges is that biblical exegesis fulfills, in the Church and in the world, an *indispensable task*. To attempt to by-pass it when seeking to understand the Bible would be to create an illusion and display lack of respect for the inspired Scripture.

When fundamentalists relegate exegetes to the role of translators only (failing to grasp that translating the Bible is already a work of exegesis) and refuse to follow them further in their studies, these same fundamentalists do not realize that, for all their very laudable concern for total fidelity to the Word of

God, they proceed in fact along ways which will lead them far away from the true meaning of the biblical texts, as well as from full acceptance of the consequences of the Incarnation. The eternal Word became incarnate at a precise period of history, within a clearly defined cultural and social environment. Anyone who desires to understand the Word of God should humbly seek it out there where it has made itself visible and accept to this end the necessary help of human knowledge. Addressing men and women, from the beginnings of the Old Testament onward, God made use of all the possibilities of human language, while at the same time accepting that his word be subject to the constraints caused by the limitations of this language. Proper respect for inspired Scripture requires undertaking all the labors necessary to gain a thorough grasp of its meaning. Certainly, it is not possible that each Christian personally pursue all the kinds of research which make for a better understanding of the biblical text. This task is entrusted to exegetes, who have the responsibility in this matter to see that all profit from their labor.

A second conclusion is that the very nature of biblical texts means that interpreting them will require continued use of the *historical-critical method,* at least in its principal procedures. The Bible, in effect, does not present itself as a direct revelation of timeless truths but as the written testimony to a series of interventions in which God reveals himself in human history. In a way that differs from tenets of other religions, the message of the Bible is solidly grounded in history. It follows that the biblical writings cannot be correctly understood without an examination of the historical circumstances that shaped them. "Diachronic" research will always be indispensable for exegesis. Whatever be their own interest and value, "synchronic" approaches cannot replace it. To function in a way that will be fruitful, synchronic approaches should accept the conclusions of the diachronic, at least according to their main lines.

But, granted this basic principle, the synchronic approaches (the rhetorical, narrative, semiotic and others) are capable, to some extent at least, of bringing about a renewal of exegesis and making a very useful contribution. The historical-critical method, in fact, cannot lay claim to enjoying a monopoly in this area. It must be conscious of *its limits,* as well as of the dangers to which it is exposed. Recent developments in philosophical hermeneutics and, on the other hand, the observations which we have been able to make concerning interpretation within the Biblical Tradition and the Tradition of the Church have shed light upon many aspects of the problem of interpretation that the historical-critical method has tended to ignore. Concerned above all to establish the meaning of texts by situating them in their original historical context, this method has at times shown itself insufficiently attentive to the dynamic aspect of meaning and to the possibility that meaning can continue to develop. When historical-critical exegesis does not go as far as to take into account the final result of the editorial process but remains absorbed solely in the issues of sources and stratification of texts, it fails to bring the exegetical task to completion.

Through fidelity to the great Tradition, of which the Bible itself is a witness, Catholic exegesis should avoid as much as possible this kind of professional bias and maintain its identity as a *theological discipline,* the principal aim of which is the deepening of faith. This does not mean a lesser involvement in scholarly research of the most rigorous kind, nor should it provide excuse for abuse of methodology out of apologetic concern. Each sector of research (textual criticism, linguistic study, literary analysis, etc.) has its own proper rules, which it ought follow with full autonomy. But no one of these specializations is an end in itself. In the organization of the exegetical task as a whole, the orientation toward the principal goal should remain paramount and thereby serve to obviate any waste of energy. Catholic exegesis does not have the right to become lost, like a stream of water, in the sands of a hypercritical analysis. Its task is to fulfill, in the Church and in the world, a vital function, that of contributing to an ever more authentic transmission of the content of the inspired Scriptures.

The work of Catholic exegesis already tends toward this end, hand in hand with the renewal of other theological disciplines and with the pastoral task of actualizing and inculturating of the Word of God. In examining the present state of the question and expressing some reflections on the matter, the present essay hopes to have made some contribution toward the gaining, on the part of all, of a clearer awareness of the role of the Catholic exegete.

Rome, April 15, 1993

BOOKS & MEDIA

The Daughters of St. Paul operate book and media centers at the following addresses. Visit, call or write the one nearest you today, or find us on the World Wide Web, www.pauline.org

CALIFORNIA
3908 Sepulveda Blvd, Culver City, CA 90230 — 310-397-8676
2640 Broadway Street, Redwood City, CA 94063 — 650-369-4230
5945 Balboa Avenue, San Diego, CA 92111 — 858-565-9181

FLORIDA
145 S.W. 107th Avenue, Miami, FL 33174 — 305-559-6715

HAWAII
1143 Bishop Street, Honolulu, HI 96813 — 808-521-2731
Neighbor Islands call: 866-521-2731

ILLINOIS
172 North Michigan Avenue, Chicago, IL 60601 — 312-346-4228

LOUISIANA
4403 Veterans Memorial Blvd, Metairie, LA 70006 — 504-887-7631

MASSACHUSETTS
885 Providence Hwy, Dedham, MA 02026 — 781-326-5385

MISSOURI
9804 Watson Road, St. Louis, MO 63126 — 314-965-3512

NEW JERSEY
561 U.S. Route 1, Wick Plaza, Edison, NJ 08817 — 732-572-1200

NEW YORK
150 East 52nd Street, New York, NY 10022 — 212-754-1110

PENNSYLVANIA
9171-A Roosevelt Blvd, Philadelphia, PA 19114 — 215-676-9494

SOUTH CAROLINA
243 King Street, Charleston, SC 29401 — 843-577-0175

TENNESSEE
4811 Poplar Avenue, Memphis, TN 38117 — 901-761-2987

TEXAS
114 Main Plaza, San Antonio, TX 78205 — 210-224-8101

VIRGINIA
1025 King Street, Alexandria, VA 22314 — 703-549-3806

CANADA
3022 Dufferin Street, Toronto, ON M6B 3T5 — 416-781-9131

¡También somos su fuente para libros, videos y música en español!